AMOUR

# Amour

## How the French Talk About Love

### STEFANIA ROUSSELLE

PENGUIN BOOKS

PENGUIN BOOKS

An imprint of Penguin Random House LLC

penguinrandomhouse.com

Copyright © 2020 by Stefania Rousselle
Penguin supports copyright. Copyright fuels creativity, encourages diverse voices,
promotes free speech, and creates a vibrant culture. Thank you for buying an authorized edition
of this book and for complying with copyright laws by not reproducing, scanning, or distributing any
part of it in any form without permission. You are supporting writers and allowing Penguin to
continue to publish books for every reader.

ISBN 9780143134534 (hardcover)
ISBN 9780525506324 (ebook)
Printed in China

1 3 5 7 9 10 8 6 4 2

*Book Design by Claire Vaccaro*

*For Rolande*

# INTRODUCTION

It was Friday night. I was at home, in my pj's, on my couch, watching a documentary, *Reporters*, by Raymond Depardon. But then an alert popped up on my phone: "Hostages taken at the Bataclan in Paris." In a second, I was out in the street. And I saw it: the fear, the police, the ambulances.

It was November 13, 2015. A massacre was taking place right down my street at the Bataclan concert hall. Terrorists were blowing themselves up and shooting people all over Paris.

I ran back up to my apartment, grabbed my camera gear, and started recording.

My editor at the *New York Times* called.

"Are you on it?"

"Yes."

I hadn't even had time to change out of my pj's.

I had been working as a freelance video journalist for the *New York Times* for the past five years. I covered sex slavery in Spain. The European debt crisis and families' despair. Pain and sadness.

I also covered fashion in Paris, Milan, and London. Trauma versus glitter. Always on deadline. Always working in a rush. Film, edit, leave. Film, edit, leave. Pain, sadness, despair, repeat.

Back at home, I needed comfort. But I would never get it: "What you did is not enough," my partner would say. I was never good enough. Ever. He injected his poison. Constantly. And I let it in; I was too in love with him. When I was at my lowest, he left me. His job was done. I was dead inside.

But I had to focus. I had work to do. I didn't want to let anyone down. "I am strong." I could do this. "Go Stefania, go. Work."

But then the Paris attacks happened. That terrible night in November 2015. 130 dead and 413 wounded. A man I knew died at the concert hall. I remembered dancing with him that very summer at a friend's wedding. But he was gone now. Shot by a terrorist. The sadness overwhelmed me.

For weeks, whenever I heard sirens in the middle of the night, I would jump out of bed and start packing my camera gear, thinking I needed to go out and report. I couldn't stop. I had to work. "I am strong."

The stories kept piling up. I embedded with France's far-right party—the National Front. The party was very close to winning the regional elections, and I was there to witness it. Cover the hate. The racism. More poison. But I couldn't blink; I was a journalist.

Truth is, I was broken. I was suffocating. My heart was crushed. I had stopped believing in love. I wanted to die.

I would stay in the dark. In my room. For months.

But I decided to give myself one last chance. Because deep inside of me, there was hope. I told myself that I was going to go look for this so-called love. I was going to see for myself if people really cared for each other. Or if love was just a lie.

So I got in my car and hit the road.

I had no idea where to start. Then I thought of my grandmother, Maria, who was born in Hungary. Her stepfather ran a hospital there. Toward the end of World War II, the Soviet Army invaded her country and killed everyone in its way. She had to escape. Her family finally found refuge in a garage close to Nuremberg. But they had nothing, and her grandmother starved to death so everyone else could eat. But they were still hungry, so my grandmother was sent to get provisions. She went to the American base. And there was Henry, my grandfather, an intelligence officer with the Office of Strategic Services. They fell in love. Before long, my mother was born.

The north of France. That's where I was going to head. To the refugee camps in Calais. But when I got there, nothing was left of them. The president had decided to tear them down to stop migrants from settling. So they had to hide in the woods. Sleep in the mud. Hoping to reach the United Kingdom. I arrived on a day when the police refused to let nongovernmental organizations (NGOs) do their lunch distribution. Not even water. I remember hundreds of hungry people, with loads of food right in front of them. Not being able to touch it. A few hours later, the police finally allowed the NGOs to serve dinner. Refugees crawled out of the forest like zombies and got in line. I walked up to Salam Salar, a thirty-one-year-old man from Pakistan. I told him about my grandmother and the journey I was starting in search of love. What he said boggled me: "Love is my mother. Love is in trees and flowers. Love is good. I have a wife and four children, but they weren't able to come to France with me. I miss them." He was seeing love around him, even in the worst conditions possible.

I didn't have a plan. No structure. No meetings. No agenda. I just wanted to wander. Get lost. Reconnect with people. The same day I met Salam, I sat down with Edith, a fifty-four-year-old accountant, in her impeccable white house in Sangatte, near Calais. She sighed: "I am in love with the idea of love. I think it is a noble feeling. But when will I actually feel it? I have been with a man for a couple of years now, and I break up with him every day. But then, every night, he comes back. I am too much of a coward to leave him. I am so scared of solitude." It was brutal. People were pure. They were raw. There was no pathos. No bullshit. I remember Marcel, a sixty-three-year-old shepherd I met in the Pyrenees. We got so drunk together. When I told the people in the village I was going to look for him up in the valley, they all told me: "Get some pastis," a delicious anise-flavored liqueur. And I did. I poured it into a plastic bottle so it wouldn't be heavy in my backpack and hiked up to find him. And when I did, we shared the bottle. He had named his cabin the Villa of Those Deprived of Love because he was the least favorite child in his family. When he started talking about his wife, Katia, there was no romanticism. "Do I love her? I don't know. *Love* is a weird word. I care about Katia. That must be love. She cares about me too—a bit too much."

Marie-Elisabeth. Pierre. Andrée. Annick. Michel. Claire. Patrick. For each beautiful and consoling moment, there was one of abandonment. Of loss or rejection. Of despair. Like Lucien, an eighty-two-year-old retired mason, whom I met in a little town in the southwest of France. His wife,

Marie-Jeanne, had just died: "In the winter, we would watch television, then sit near the fire and fall asleep in our respective chairs. We were happy. I always hoped it would last forever. It didn't."

I felt the extreme solitude of people. The extreme anxiety to make ends meet. We are unbearably fragile. Incredibly complex. We fear others, we doubt our ability to be loved. Still, there was resilience. Love kept them going.

And they gave me a lot. I slept under the roof of nearly all the people I met. I wanted to feel surrounded and to be with people. So I decided to rent rooms in people's homes. Not only did they open their homes to me but also their hearts. Their most intimate space. Their cocoon. The place where they grow old, laugh, cry, raise kids. We cooked food and drank wine. We cried and laughed together. They introduced me to their friends and their family. We watched TV. Walked the dogs. They taught me how to milk goats. How they grew their vegetables. How they raised their bulls. I went fishing and got seasick. I even spent Christmas with them. I loved waking up in the morning in my pj's and walking into their kitchens, with the smell of coffee. The *pain au chocolat* on the table. The cats jumping on the counter. The kids screaming because they didn't want to go to school.

The power of connecting. The lightness of being. The mundanity of life.

After a few days, it was time to go. I would get back in my car. Put the radio on and hit the road. Suburbs. Towns. Beaches. Plains. Villages. Moissac. Ernestviller. Andel. Le Vauclin. Blaceret.

And I would go from heart to heart. Yann. Alexandre. Charlotte. Gérard. Christian. Suzy. Amélie. Noé. Nicolas. Lucile.

What follows is their gift to us.

They mended my heart. I hope they mend yours. This is not just a portrait of the French; it is a portrait of all of us.

Yes, we are imperfect beings, but we have something that links us together, and that is sublime: Love. *Amour.*

AMOUR

# SHEETS

*Mézidon-Canon, Calvados*

I was a widow. I was lonely. I was starting to feel tired. I didn't speak to anyone. I was alone with my TV. I'd had enough.

On a Wednesday, I took my car and went to the restaurant. Claude was there, sad, eating in a corner. I went up to him and asked: "Are you okay?" He said yes. I asked him: "Can I sit with you?" He said yes. I paid for his meal. I told him: "You're going to come to my house, and I'll make you some coffee."

I waited for him. He had a meeting with his insurance company, so he couldn't come right away. I couldn't wait to see him. I was standing by the window. I saw cars coming. I was thinking: "No, not this one. Not this one."

Suddenly, there he was. My heart was beating. I was happy. He came in, I took him in my arms, and I kissed him. He had kept his word.

I told him: "Come for lunch tomorrow at noon."

On Thursdays, my daughter comes to clean my house. I said: "We need to change the sheets, and we are going to put on my satin sheets." I have blue and pink ones. I chose the pink ones.

That day, we made love for the first time. He never left. We have been together for three years now. My first husband hit me. The second died of an epilepsy attack.

I love this fool.

*Rolande Mignot (February 13, 1944–June 5, 2018), cleaning lady and cook, and Claude Vinandy, 78, retired dairy driver*

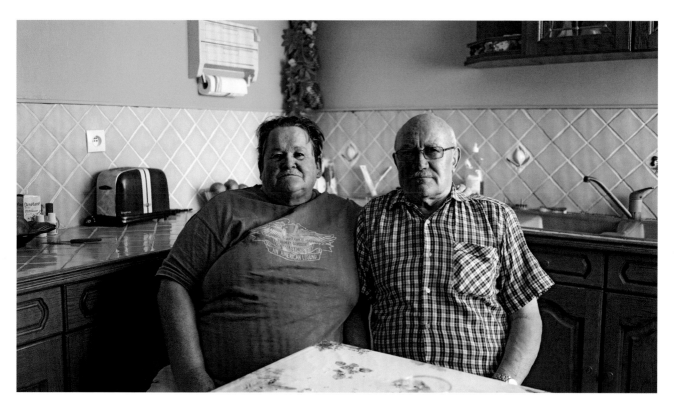

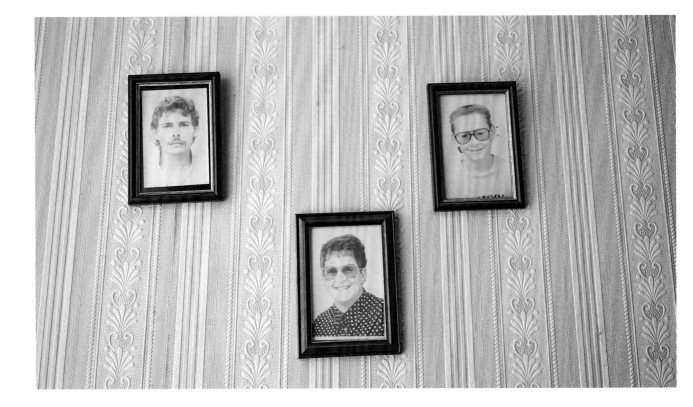

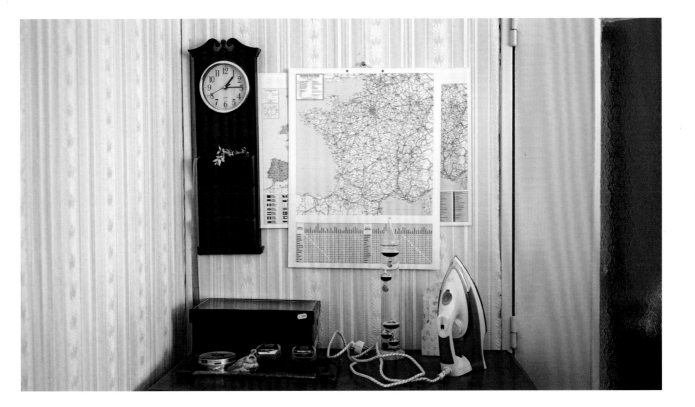

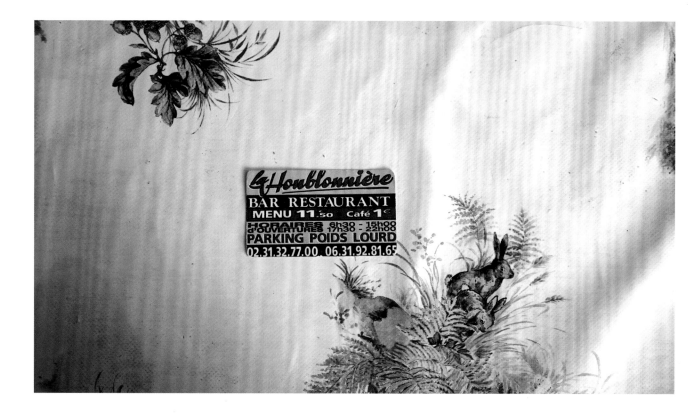

La Houblonnière
BAR RESTAURANT
MENU 11.50   Café 1€
HORAIRES 6h30 - 15h00
d'OUVERTURES 17h30 - 22h00
PARKING POIDS LOURD
02.31.32.77.00  06.31.92.81.65

Sheets

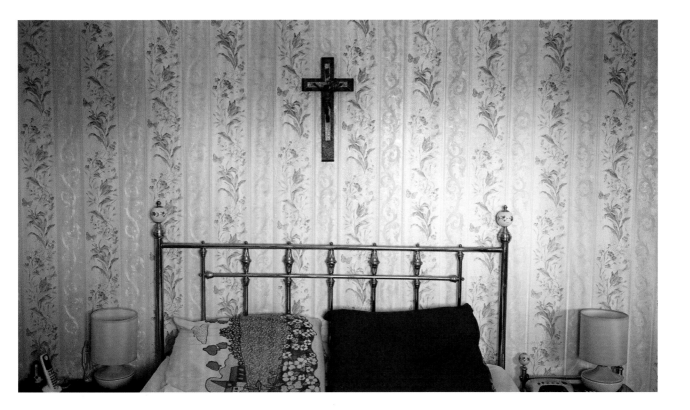

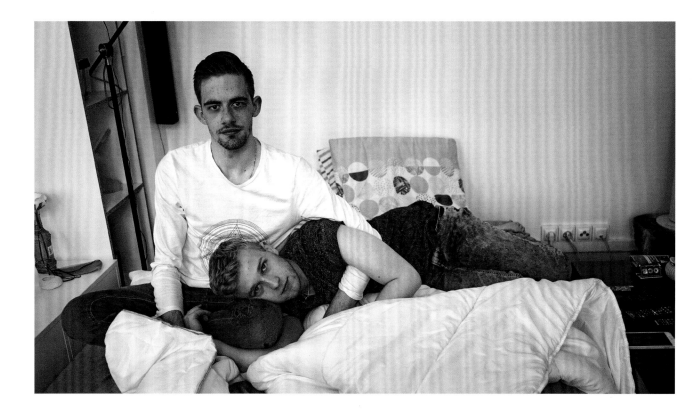

# Bath

*Elbeuf, Seine-Maritime*

Alexandre and I met on Facebook through friends. We then talked on Skype for two months, and we fell in love.

Alexandre was kicked out of his house, and he came to live with me and my family. My parents were not aware that we were in love or that I was gay. But my mother guessed it because we looked at each other lovingly. One day, she searched my room and found all the letters we wrote each other.

In my family, we don't speak about our feelings. She had a hard time accepting it. The day she gave me her blessing, I immediately asked Alexandre to marry me. We got married two weeks ago. We are the second gay couple to get married in Elbeuf.

*Yann Désaubry, 21, marketing manager*

I decided to take Yann's last name. I am completely estranged from my family, except for my father, but he died in April. I was brought up in a foster family that I've since taken to court for mistreatment. And when I finally went back to my mother's house, she ended up throwing me out because I was gay. Today, I am at peace. With Yann, I feel confident. I love Yann's body and his childish side. I am always doing little things for him, like every night I pour him a bath and light candles, and I bring him breakfast in bed. We want at least four children.

*Alexandre Désaubry, 21, cleaning company owner*

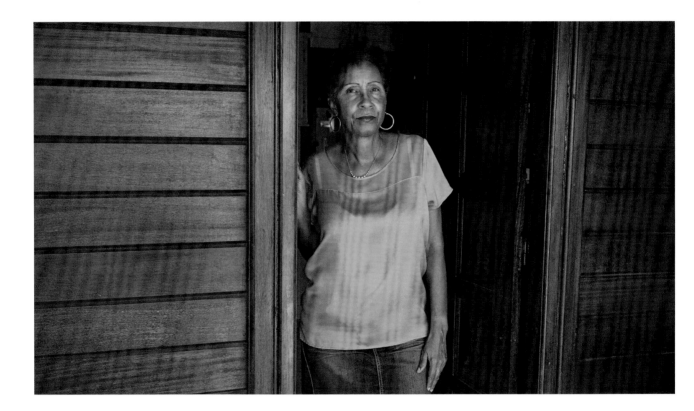

# MISTRESS

*Trois-Rivières, Guadeloupe*

When I was young, I didn't want to get married. It scared me. I didn't want to commit. It would mean belonging to someone. And I was very attached to my freedom.

But then I met him. I was twenty-seven. He was twenty-five. I was so in love. He was a rebel. I liked that. I decided to go on holiday for a month, and when I came back, he told me he had gotten engaged. I was in shock. I thought it was just a fling, that he would get back with me. But no. He married her.

Five years later, we bumped into each other at the beach. I couldn't help it; the feelings were still there. He was getting a divorce, and he asked me out. I said yes. "Here we go again," I thought. We kissed that night. It was so good. It was beautiful. I asked him to marry me. He said yes. But nothing happened. And then, we kept breaking up and getting back together again.

Until he asked to have a baby. He said he couldn't be with a woman he didn't have a child with. I was thirty-eight. Nine months later, our daughter was born.

We started living together. But he didn't always sleep at home. And after a while, he told me he needed to move to a house closer to his job. Fine. I accepted it.

One day, a woman came knocking at my door—saying she was his girlfriend. I got so nervous, I started having my period, right there in front of her. There was so much blood.

Still, I stayed by him. I couldn't get myself to leave him. And it was on and off again.

On and off.

And each time I would try to date another man, he would beg me to take him back.

After seventeen years of chaos, I just couldn't do it anymore.

I learned he got married again. Why didn't he ever marry me? Sometimes I wonder whether I was ever his true girlfriend or if I had always been his mistress.

*Marie-Elisabeth Glandor, 58, school secretary*

Mistress

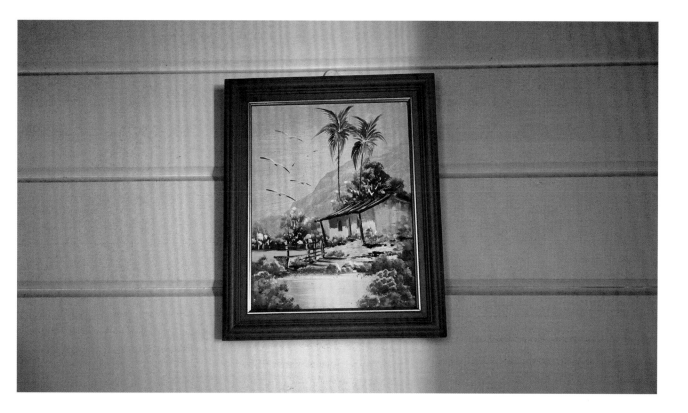

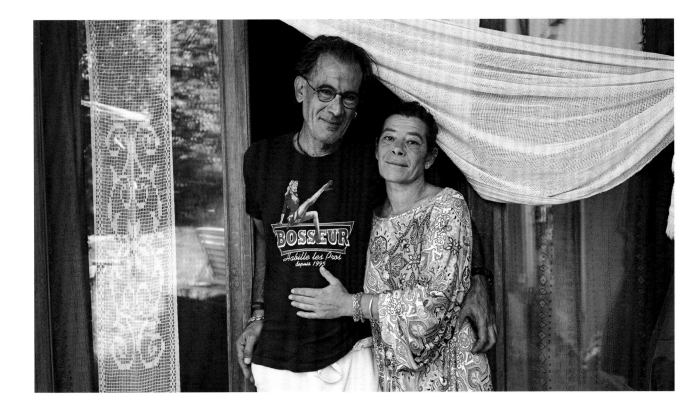

# FREE

*Barret-sur-Méouge, Hautes-Alpes*

This is the story of the waitress that gets with the boss. The best friend that becomes the bitch. And all the bad things that go with it.

But we fell in love.

Pablo and his wife were my best friends. I had known them for fifteen years. They had a snack bar, and I was the waitress. Pablo and I spent a lot of time together. We spoke a lot. And at that point in our lives, both of us were in distress.

I loved my husband. He had a beautiful heart. But I was forty-five years old. I had met him when I was seventeen. I was bored. Everything was always the same. He was a homebody. A DIYer around the house. Gardening. Picking mushrooms. Planning family reunions. Watching TV.

He was a good man. But he was killing me with all his love. It made it hard to leave him. I was on antidepressants. I had lost fifty-five pounds in a year. I felt this was it. This was my life. I had a house, I had had a beautiful wedding, I had money.

My friends said I had everything. I didn't.

I didn't have anything.

One night, I was at the snack bar with Pablo. Everyone left. And it happened. We had sex. But it wasn't sex. We actually made love, which was so disturbing. We didn't expect that at all.

Three months later, we let the cat out of the bag. We left our partners and stayed together. It was undeniable. We were going to leave them anyway. Together or not.

He became a mailman. I work at the post office. It's been a year and a half. We love to laugh. He is crazy.

When I wake up in the morning, open my eyes and see him, I am happy.

I am free again.

*Valérie Garric, 49, post office employee,
and Pablo Harrispe, 57, mail carrier*

# CAR

*Moissac, Tarn-et-Garonne*

My ex-wife kicked me out of our house. She wouldn't let me see my children. She wouldn't let me take any of my belongings. I became depressed. It was so hard to do anything. I lived out of my car. Since I was a property developer, I would also squat in apartments I was building.

I was cut off from the world.

My ex-wife wanted to slaughter me. Not seeing my children was terrible. This happens to so many men, and we are powerless.

I was seeing all these online ads for dating sites. So I just went for it, and I met Emmanuelle. We would write to each other all the time. She didn't care that I lived out of a car.

It quickly changed into love. We have been together for seven years.

Emmanuelle got pregnant. We would never talk about it. She didn't want a child. Neither did I. I couldn't see my children, so how could I have another one?

But then, Victor was born. Once we saw him, it changed everything. He put purpose back into our lives.

When my two girls found out they had a baby brother, they put pressure on their mother to meet him. I hadn't seen them for four and a half years.

If it weren't for him, it would not have worked. He is the bridge.

*Patrick Celard, 53, stay-at-home dad,*
*and Emmanuelle Lemée, 44, timber negotiator*

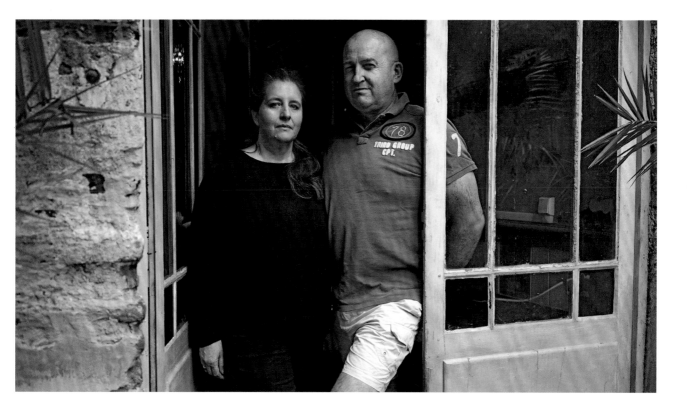

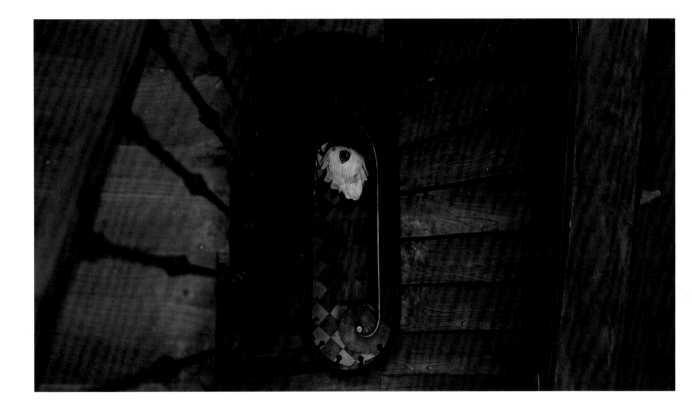

Car

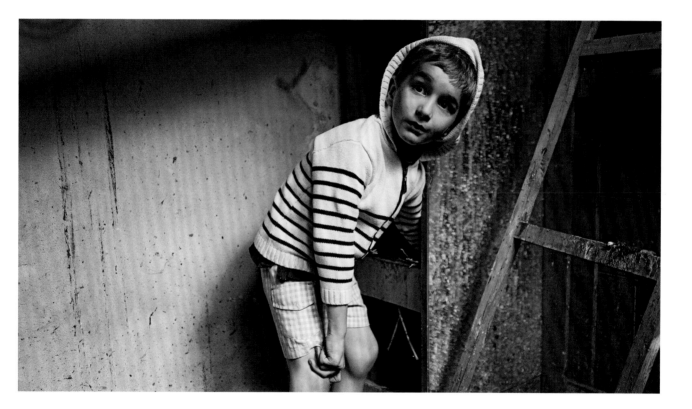

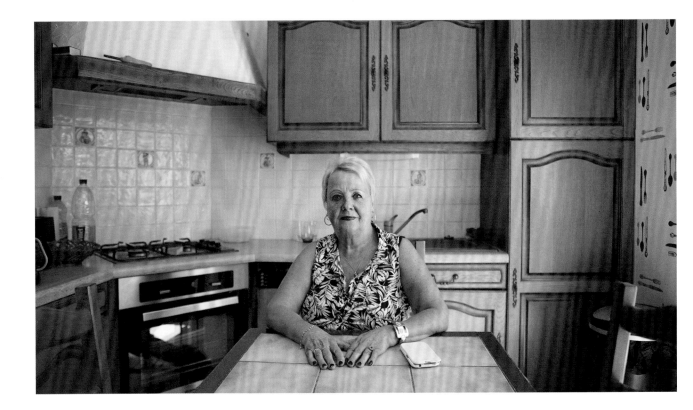

# GRAVES

*Dunkirk, Nord*

I met Michel in school. I was twelve.

Later, we worked in the same textile factory. Then he went to work at the port, as a docker. We were married for thirty years.

He was rather withdrawn. Not jovial like I am. He didn't like to dance. But he was a good father, and he was so handsome.

He died. Cancer got him. When he got sick, he changed. He was no longer the man I had known. He became so mean. He didn't have vocal cords anymore, so his words sounded even harsher. They were coming out from the esophagus. He was just suffering so much. It was terrible.

I learned to live again. I became a cleaning lady. A waitress. It kept me busy. There were my kids too, but they had their own lives.

I decided to go dancing again, at a venue people call the Widows' Ball. I met Alain there. He was so amusing. Gentle. Tender. But I couldn't tell him "I love you" as I'd told Michel. It wasn't the same.

He died too. A couple months ago.

Today, I go see my two lovers at their graves. Alain's death is recent, so I go to the cemetery once a month and put a flower on his headstone. My husband, I go see him three times a year: on his birthday, Father's Day, and All Saints' Day.

I have had only one love in my life, and that was Michel. I loved him passionately. He was my man. What do I miss about him the most? His kisses. They made me climb to seventh heaven.

*Marlène Duchemin, 66, retired cleaning lady*

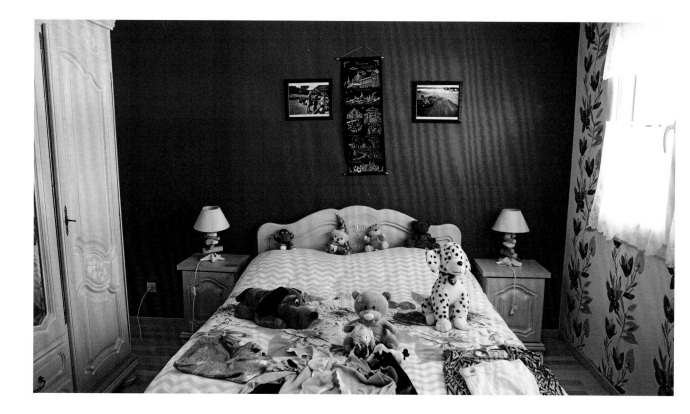

GRAVES

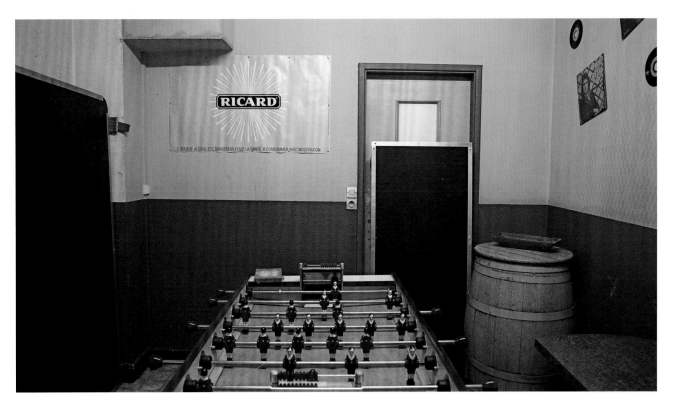

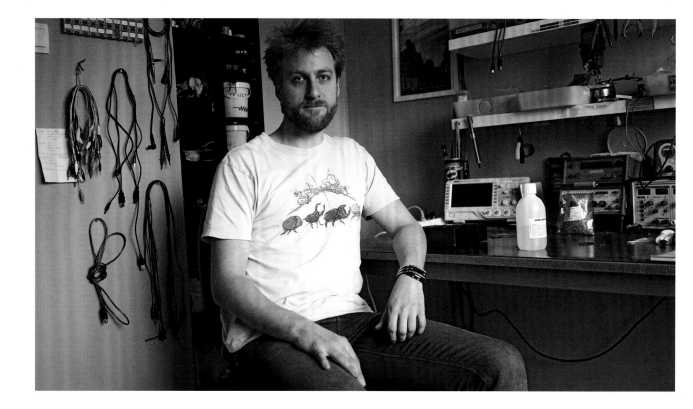

# DUST

*Ernestviller, Moselle*

I am a nurse in a psychiatric hospital, a special unit where they put the most violent people. *Normality*, I don't know what that means.

I was always the shy one. The one who was in love but never shared his feelings. The one who went only with the girls who seduced me, not the ones I wanted.

I am an adult today. I am not super at ease with people. I always feel out of step with them. I do not feel rejected, but the feeling of loneliness has always been very present in my life.

I like the idea that substance is made of emptiness and that particles never actually touch each other. It's exactly like the social masks that we wear. It's so hard to really get to know someone. Authenticity is extremely rare.

I don't like one-night stands. I've had some, but I get attached too fast and too much. I am hypersensitive. I have so much to give.

Love is like the dust of eternity: you never forget the memories, those tiny treasures.

My girlfriend left me two weeks ago. We had been together for one year. Our relationship was like a plant: each time there was a sprout, she would pull it out, because she didn't want our love to grow.

This morning, I just didn't know what to do with myself. I played video games; I quit right away. I started a movie; I stopped it. I started a book, and I put it right down. I keep thinking about her. She had a particular smell. It was her smell.

I have been crying a lot lately.

*Pierre Vilhem, 34, nurse*

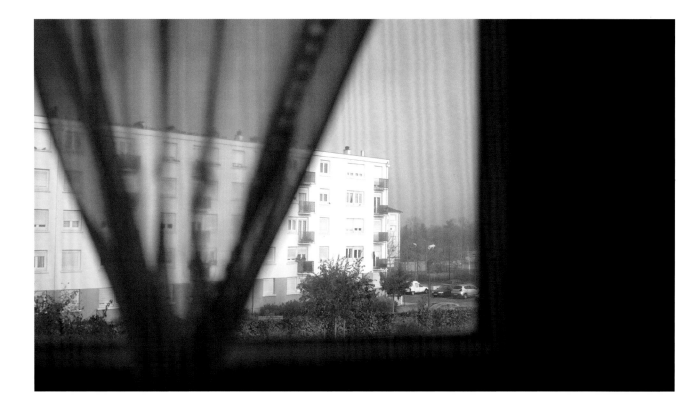

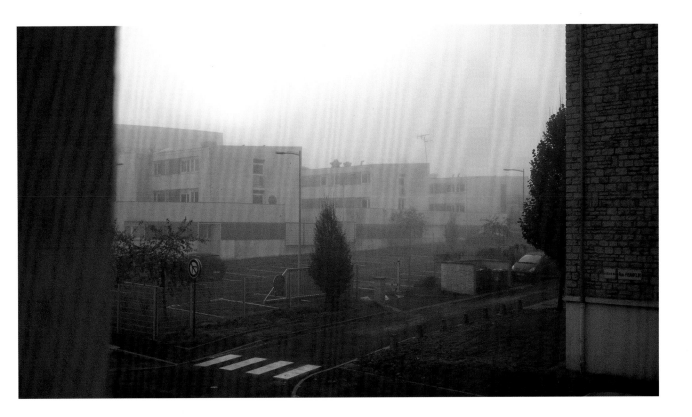

# Roots

*Pau, Pyrénées-Atlantiques*

He moved to my street when I was eight years old—three houses down from mine. I liked him right away. One of our neighbors would say: "When Nora grows up, she will marry Olivier."

At fourteen, I thought: "I really want to kiss him." He was wild, not interested in girls. He had a bad boy side to him. He used to get into fights. He was the only white boy in our school, so he was picked on a lot.

He used to do woodwork in a workshop. I would go and pretend to be interested in what he was doing. We kissed once, and the next day he told me I was too young. And then one year later, at a party, a guy told him I was cute, and that's when it clicked. I was fifteen and a half. He was nineteen. At that age, you're so small but feel so grown up. I remember he once left his sweater behind, and I would dig my face into it. It smelled so good.

We've been together for twenty-three years, and we have two girls. I am so proud.

I have never been with another man. He is not my best friend. He is my man. I don't like to say "my husband." "My man" is more physical. In friendship, there is no physical aspect. We send each other naughty texts. We even have special codes for special words.

I'm in love with the simplicity of our daily life. He is my soul mate. When he is not there, I'm not myself. But we are not fused together either. Fusion is prison. We had a time when we were wrapped up in each other, in our bubble. And that wasn't the best part of our relationship.

The best part is the complicity that came with the years, the way we understand each other. It's our roots that are tangled together. And that is stronger and more intense than the passion we had.

*Nora Merle, 38, human resources manager*

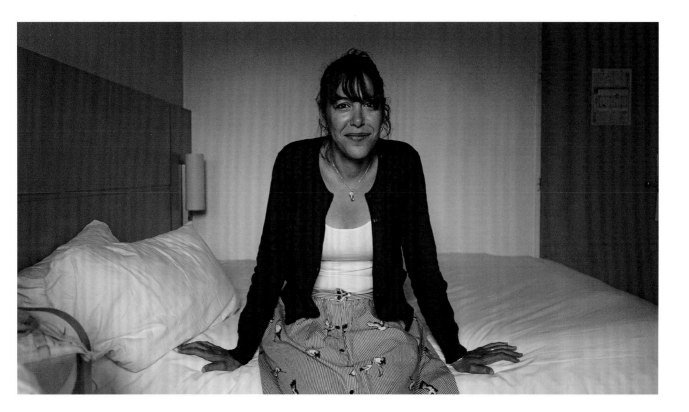

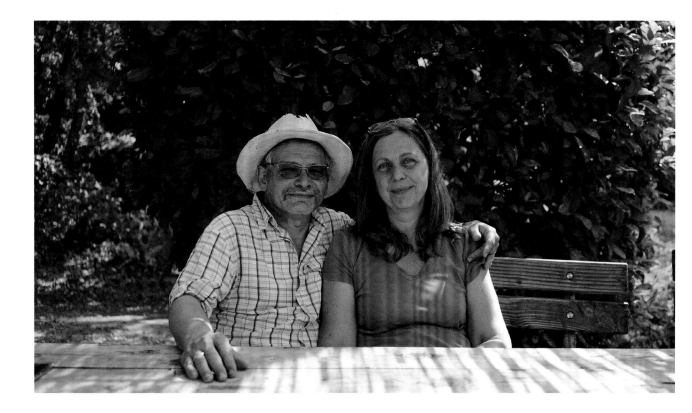

# SALT

*Viens, Vaucluse*

We were in the same parish. We were students. It was called the Salt Shaker, and we were the Salt of the Earth. We wanted to give taste to people's lives. Michel already had his mustache. He was in charge of the group. And I would listen to him—passionately. One night, we kissed.

It has never been easy.

I had six pregnancies but only three children. I suffered with depression that I didn't treat.

And Michel fell in love with another woman.

I had grown up with the image of the prince on his white horse: all of that wasn't true. I suffered. A lot.

But Michel was the man I loved, the man I had chosen. I couldn't pretend he was someone he wasn't. His heart was free; he always had been fundamentally free. And that's why I had fallen in love with him. So I chose to stay.

Yes, I was tempted to leave. I could have had other lives. Other men. But love is a continuous series of choices. Of renunciation. Maybe I was too stubborn. Maybe I was too obstinate. But I was consistent.

He stayed too.

We had to fight to get back our density, our dialogue, our affection and tenderness. Because it was all gone. We dug deep in our hearts, because we knew there was still beauty in "us."

I realized something that changed me forever. I had always been searching for solidity in him, but the only place I could find it was within me.

Today, we are celebrating our thirty-fourth anniversary. Michel always says it's hard to know whether we are happy. We say we have our moments of happiness. We cultivate them. We go sleep by a creek and wake up at sunrise to swim in the sea. We put three candles out on our porch, light up a cigar, and drink a good rum under the stars. Tomorrow, the kids are coming over, and we are going to cook lamb all together.

You see, I never believed in forgiveness. I always believed in healing.

*Annick Grégoire, 54, psychologist,*
*and Michel Grégoire, 56, engineer*

# SHAME

*Ouanne, Yonne*

I was born with arthrogryposis, a muscle and joint condition that left my arms twisted.

But the pain has never been in my arms. It has always been mental, and I was always afraid of getting rejected by girls. Since I was working as an entertainment manager, I found a way of compensating my shame: money. I had a lot, and I wanted to impress the girls with it.

It's all fine and well to say that being handicapped doesn't matter. But it is not true: People reject you. People turn their back on you. You feel like a nobody. I got used to being slapped in the face, and at a certain point I just went with the flow. If it worked, good. If it didn't, too bad.

With Nadia, there was none of that. I met her on a ski tow. She had lost one of her skis, and I brought it back to her. We decided to meet for a drink, and we made love that night.

She never left me.

She brought me back together. She boosted my morale. She made me feel I existed. It's been twenty-eight years. And we have two kids.

We are just like any other couple. We fight. We find solutions. We fight again. We find solutions.

She is my friend. She is my wife. She is my lover.

And when she talks about my handicap, she says: "It could have happened to anyone."

*Christian Cumont, 57, master of ceremonies and DJ, and Nadia Cumont, 47, nurse*

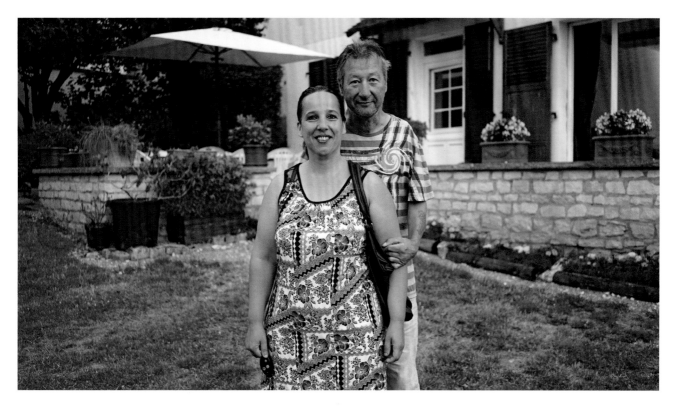

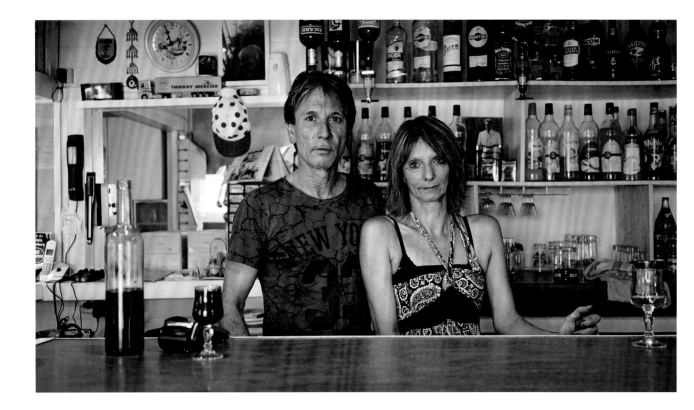

# HEART ATTACK

*Cussy-les-Forges, Yonne*

I was a truck driver for twenty-eight years.

I met her in a factory that I was working for. Each time I would stop there to fill my truck with gas, I would have coffee with her. We fell in love.

We both wanted to open a bar and settle down. So we bought this place.

She died of a heart attack one month before it opened. In the shower. She had heart problems. She was forty-two. Her name was Marie.

I wanted to fight for her, for this project we had, for our future. Thank God I had this restaurant or I would have gone back on the road, and I don't know what would have happened to me.

I'll never get over her death. I was so in love with her. Afterward, I felt guilty: Did I push her too hard with work?

It's not easy. The more failures you experience, the more difficult it is to fall in love. On the other hand, there is always something that gives you hope. It's contradictory. I'm very sentimental. And with love, I feel secure.

I am exhausted. I would like to stop thinking because it makes you suffer too much. I am in search of serenity. I'm a big fan of Johnny Hallyday, and I recognize myself in his songs.

I met Rosalia on the internet. It's been only two or three months. When we make love, we leave Earth and forget our problems. Right now, she's staying at my place with her son, as a test run. They've been here for four days. She is gentle, tender, and tolerant. But we don't know each other very well yet.

It's going to be okay. We are starting a new story.

*Jean-Luc Mollaret, 52, owner of the roadside restaurant Route 6, and Rosalia Agrestu, 49, waitress*

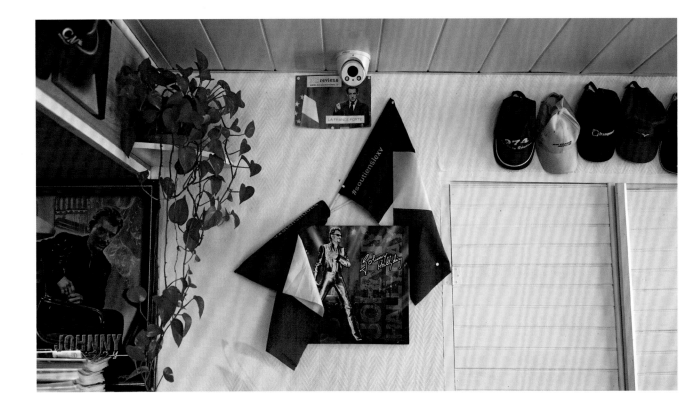

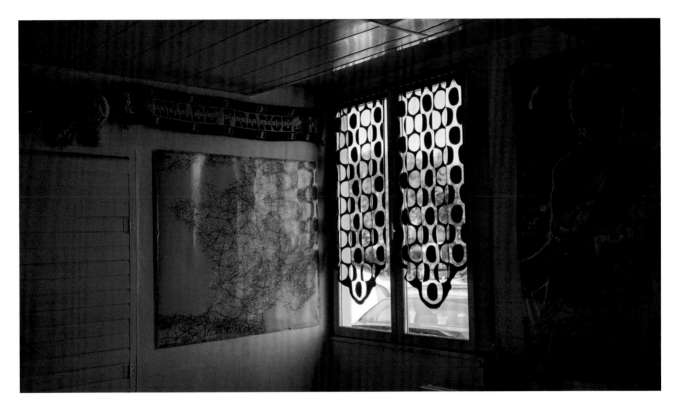

# SPARK

*Andel, Côtes-d'Armor*

I have been divorced for three years. When my son was six months old, I wanted to leave. I was bored. I was going in circles.

My wife made me feel guilty, so I stayed. It wasn't love. I stayed because of guilt.

When my son was fourteen years old, I wanted to get a divorce. But he told me: "If you divorce, you are not my father anymore."

So I stayed.

I was bored at work. I was bored with my marriage. So we decided to open a pizzeria to put the spark back in the relationship. But it faded again, quite fast.

I was married for twenty-two years without really being in love. The day of the wedding was fun, but was it the party that I loved or my wife?

I had one heartbreak. It was the end of a friendship with a man.

I am not quite sure what love is because I've never really lived it. It would probably be tenderness. I am not very sexual; I can do without.

I am a nudist, and I am going to Corsica soon. Maybe I'll find a woman on the beach there.

I didn't love myself before, and now I do.

*Pascal Grimault, 52, industrial sauce maker*

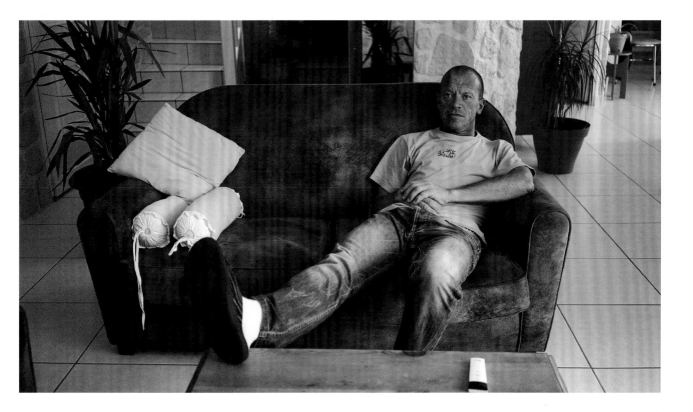

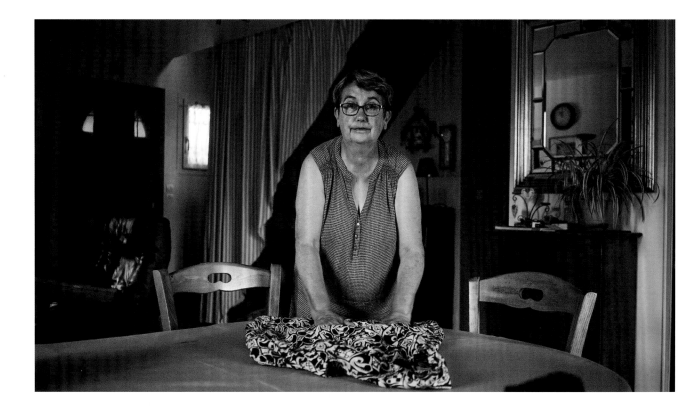

# CROSS

*Gournay-en-Bray, Seine-Maritime*

When I was thirty-eight, I was with a man who abused me.

A couple of days after the second time he raped me, he went out to get some bread and croissants. We had an event scheduled together, so I looked into his planner and saw that he had drawn a cross on that day with a note: "Made love with Chantal even though she refused." I then looked at the date of the first time he had raped me: same notation— another cross. I took a red pen and wrote: "Rape. Rape."

He had also written down what he spent on me when we went to a restaurant.

We went on a spiritual retreat together that summer. I thought it would put things back in their place, even though I knew it was over.

In September, I became pregnant. I kept the child and left him. For years afterward, he tried to turn people against me.

My son is seventeen years old now.

I never got married.

But, yes, I still believe in love. Who knows what might happen?

*Chantal Thibaut, 62, retired schoolteacher*

# COCKROACHES

*Dunkirk, Nord*

At the time, there were no mixed couples in Dunkirk. People from the village hid behind their curtains to look at us. One day, we even got arrested by the police because Justin is black. My mother rejected me and wanted to send me to a correctional facility. So I left home, with nothing, just my purse.

And when we wanted to get married, the first priest we asked refused, saying black people were like cockroaches.

We've loved each other for fifty-three years. And people now fight to get into the Caribbean nights we organize!

*Andrée Vaïty-Gruwez, 70, retired fish shop owner, and*
*Justin Vaïty-Gruwez, 82, retired industrial technician*

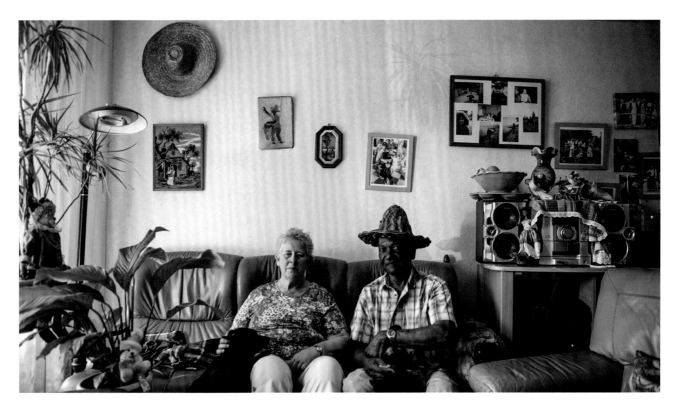

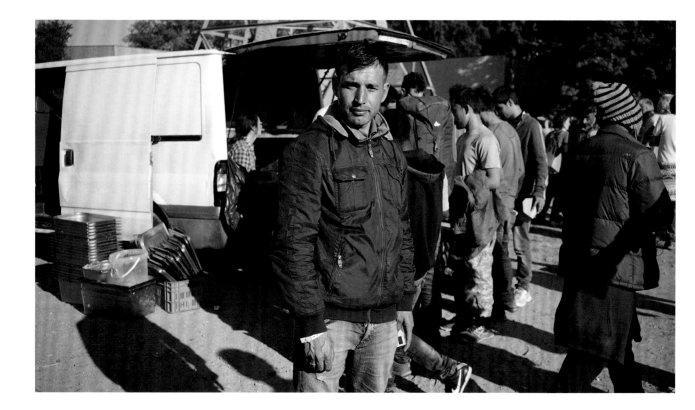

# FLOWERS

*Calais, Pas-de-Calais*

Love is my mother. Love is in trees and flowers. Love is good. I have a wife and four children, but they weren't able to come to France with me. I am from Pakistan. I miss them. When I got here, I had to go to the hospital because of a kidney stone. This is a bad life.

*Salam Salar, 31, unemployed*

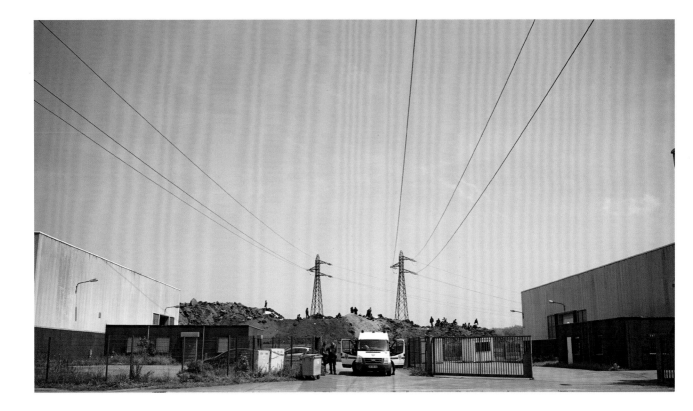

FLOWERS

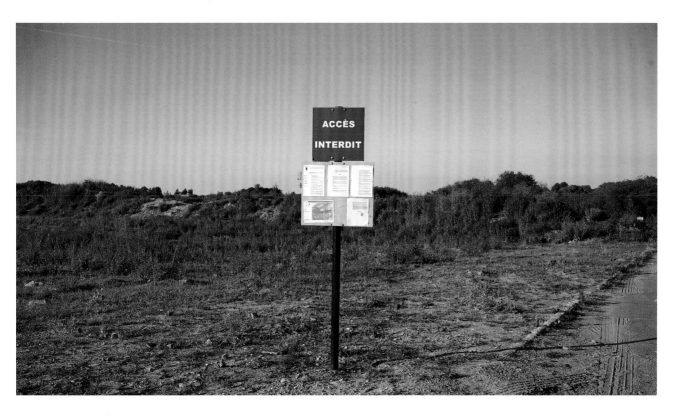

# NIGHT

*Sangatte, Nord*

I am in love with the idea of love. I think it is a noble feeling. But when will I actually feel it? I have been with a man for a couple of years now, and I break up with him every day. But then, every night, he comes back. I am too much of a coward to leave him. I am so scared of solitude.

*Edith Calais, 54, accountant*

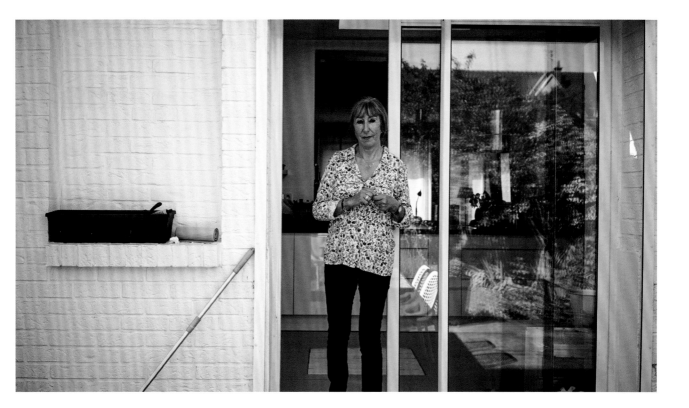

# HANDFASTING

*La Montagne, Haute-Saône*

I fell in love once with a girl. It was in Brittany. We knew about this special place with old dolmens—three big stones supporting a flat one. So one night, we carried a mattress on our heads, walked for three miles, put the mattress on top of the stones, and made love under the moonlight.

Nine months later, my baby girl was born.

But my daughter's mother didn't love me anymore and pushed me out of the house. She broke my heart. I didn't want to leave my child. So I moved to the city to be close to her. I had no money. I had to rent a room in a whorehouse—it was the cheapest place to live then.

Years passed. I was thirty-seven. I was a musician. I had all the girls I wanted. Never a problem.

But I met Miek.

And it felt like coming home.

It was more than just comfort; I think they invented the word *love* for it.

We form a team. What I don't know how to do, she does. We are stronger than one person. Her daughter is mine, and my daughter is hers. They say they are sisters.

There is something special about Miek and the way she is with people—emotional, strong, and empathetic. She is a healer. She's beautiful.

Sometimes, I sit in my rocking chair, I look around and think: "If I die now, it's okay."

*Duke van Egmond, 59, guesthouse owner*

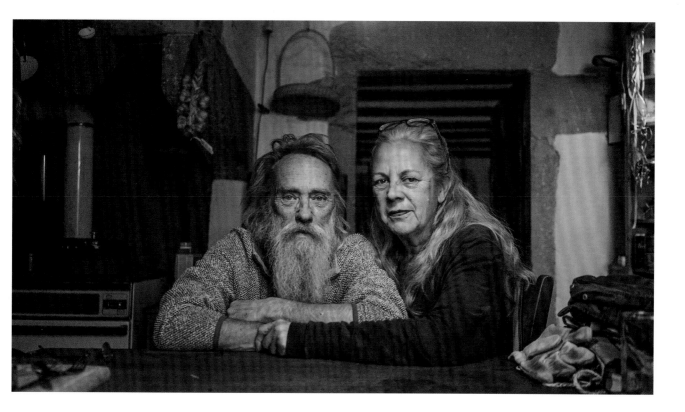

When I turned seventeen, I wanted to leave home and was looking for a way out. This American came along who was in the military, and he told me: "You are special, and I want to be with you."

I moved to the United States with him, but soon the physical and mental abuse started. I thought: "If I stay, one day somebody is going to die."

I had a child with him, hoping things would change, but that didn't work. She is handicapped. He wasn't abusive to her, but he wasn't a good father. So I got out. I left him when I was twenty-two and moved back to Holland.

Eighteen years passed. I was thinking I was going to grow old by myself, which was fine. I didn't feel incomplete.

But one night I went to a concert, and there was Duke.

We knew we were going to be together for the rest of our lives when we sat down at his home two days later. He touched my arm, and there was a flash of electricity. I had never experienced that feeling before; neither had he.

We knew.

We had an old Celtic marriage, a handfasting, where we bound our hands together with rope to symbolize commitment. It was really amazing. It still is. We moved to the mountains and built this house—together. We have been together for twenty-one years.

People say that for love to work, each person has to remain independent. But then, where is the connection? You have to dare to be dependent on the other person.

*Annemiek Couwenbergh, 62, guesthouse owner*

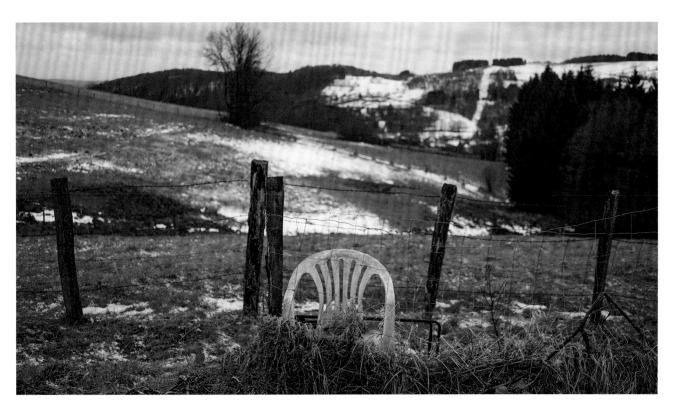

# Kiss

*Asson, Pyrénées-Atlantiques*

I have never had any partners in my life. I have never kissed a girl.

It sucks, because I am twenty-four.

My mother was depressed; I am not sure why. She didn't give me any hugs; she did not like to give warmth to other people—and so I got used to it. For me, hugging people was not very normal, and I didn't feel very comfortable with it.

I was once kissed *by* a girl; she made the move. I liked it, but it was awkward for me. I was fifteen, and I didn't really know what to do. She did everything. She could have kissed a plastic object, and it would have been the same.

To give a kiss is a more symbolic thing than to have sex. I'm not sure if it has anything to do with romance. It's a mind thing. Part of me wants to have this symbolic kiss with that one person, the mother of my children. And there is the other part, the animal side of me, that says, "Oh I don't give a fuck, just go into the club and fuck 'em all."

But then I don't do it because the first side is just stronger. I am too sensitive.

I think girls want a dominant, strong type of guy, not the sensitive man who is too emotional, like me. I am always overthinking things. I want to love one person.

I think I have waited too long now. I am afraid to fail. I have a friend who I fell in love with two years ago. I said, "I like you a lot," and she told me she liked me too, but she had another boy, and she's not a polygamist. She did not break my heart; it's more like I broke my heart. I had big expectations and put too much pressure on myself. I wrote her a poem. I was proud of it, but I've never gotten the chance to give it to her.

Most of the time, I am happy. But I am sad in the evenings. It's sad to be alone. It would be nice to sleep and wake up next to somebody and be like: "Good morning, it's gray outside."

*Philipp Zielke, 24, organic farm volunteer*

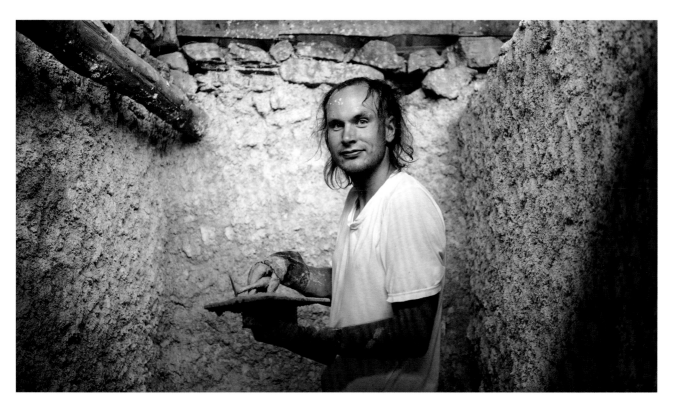

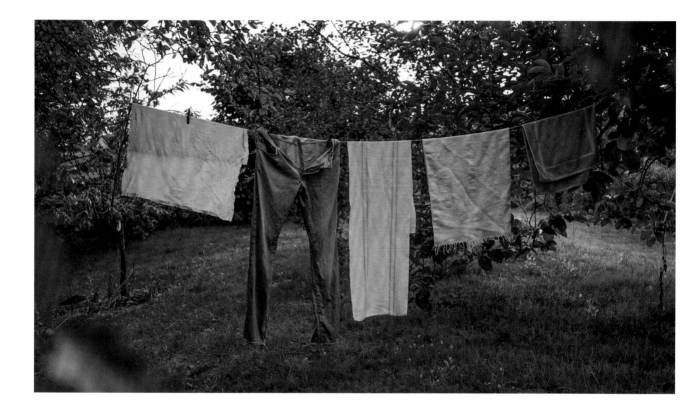

Kiss

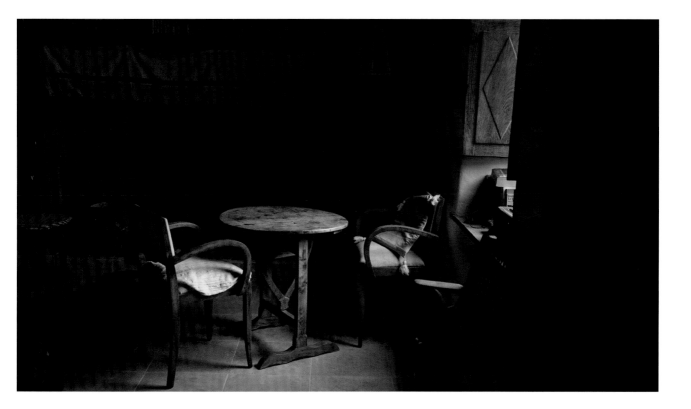

# DANCE

*Blaceret, Rhône*

When I was a young woman, I was wild. I picked up a lot of girls. I both didn't belong to anyone and belonged to everyone. I just wanted to be loved. But I had never fallen in love.

And then, I met Delphine. We were both training to become summer camp counselors. We were seventeen. We were sleeping in the same bunk bed. I was at the top. She was at the bottom. I gave her candy and played drums for her. Anything to get her attention. She had a boyfriend, but I didn't care. I wanted her.

When the training ended, we called each other every night. We fell asleep on the phone. One evening, she called me and said she was lost, confused about her feelings for me. The next day, I ditched school and picked her up after class. When I saw her, my heart was pounding. I thought, "I am in love." We went to eat pizza in the mall nearby, and then sat on a bench. She had her head on my knees. We didn't need to talk. We said good-bye, and she cried.

Delphine left her boyfriend. The first time I met him, months later, I was wearing a T-shirt and underwear. I was making waffles in Delphine's kitchen. He asked me to walk him back to the car. I thought he wanted to fight me. I was ready to punch. But he got into the car, opened his window, and said: "Please take good care of her, will you?"

I used to be a junkie and an alcoholic. When Delphine came into my life, I studied, I found a job. It's been nine years. We are in a civil union.

We love to play, run after each other like a cat and mouse. We love to dance, to lift each other up like ballet dancers in the kitchen. When she takes a shower, I sit on the stool and tell her about my day. When she is done, we swap.

Today, we are trying to have a baby. In vitro fertilization is illegal for lesbians in France, so we have to go to Spain. Delphine is on her fifth attempt. We are out of money but not out of faith.

Every night I carry her to bed. We lay down, hold each other tight, and whisper: "I love you."

*Charlotte Menet, 26, store manager,*
*and Delphine Bonny, 26, nurse*

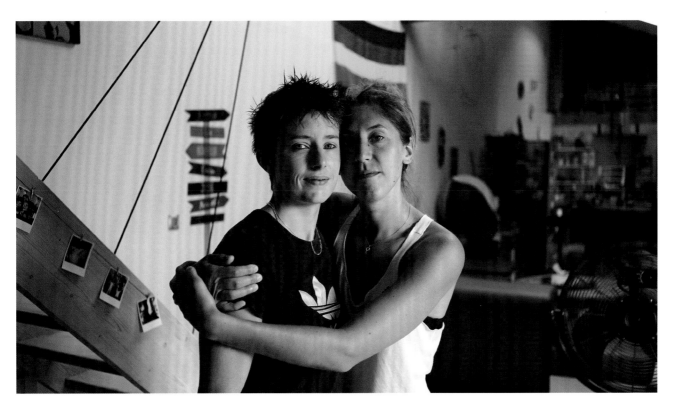

# SMOKE

*Lourmarin, Vaucluse*

I was married three times. Then I left everything to follow a radiologist who ended up leaving me for another woman. He married her. He had never wanted to marry me. I was really hurt but relieved it was over, because I was bored with him. He died just a couple of weeks ago. A stupid death, an infection he got at a hospital.

After he left me, I wasn't worried. I was sixty and still a pretty woman. It always had been easy for me, but I didn't find anyone. I've been on my own since then. It's been fifteen years. I am seventy-five now, and I no longer get attention. When you are young and attractive, everyone smiles at you. And then one day, the doors are closed. You are left alone, living with your solitude.

I used to take my car and go on road trips, alone. I just needed to take my loneliness for a stroll. I wanted to see beauty, so I went to the Camargue. To Venice. At night, in restaurants, I was by myself and felt like a complete fool. I was surrounded by grace, and there I was, alone. How sad. I decided not to travel anymore.

I still work to keep myself busy. Also, I need to, for financial reasons. I manage a wealthy man's property. It has 150 acres. There are vineyards. Gardens. There are chauffeurs, chambermaids to manage. There is so much to do. My kids are visiting me tomorrow, but my boss is here, and he won't let me stop for a week. He did say that in the evening, one of the cleaning ladies could take over if I paid half her salary. I wish I made as much as he did.

Today is Monday, and it's my day off. And like every Monday, I come to this restaurant and order aioli. I love to have a cigarette after finishing my meal. The taste of the cigarette and the garlic is so, so good. It makes me happy.

Do you mind if I smoke?

*Françoise Wyss, 75, property manager*

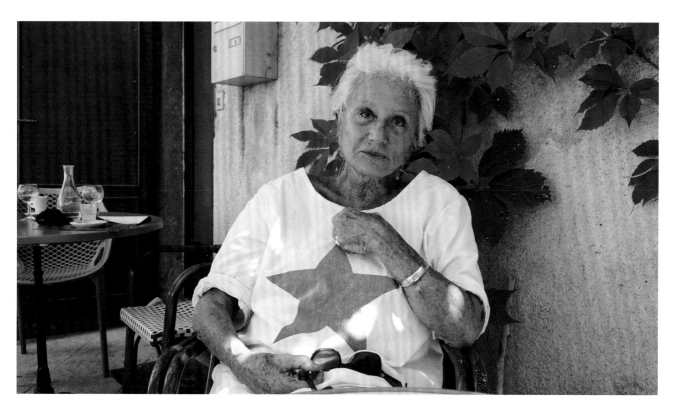

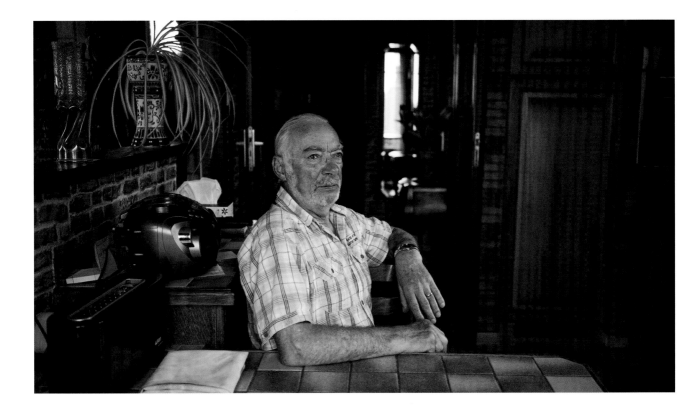

# RADIO

*Équihen-Plage, Pas-de-Calais*

I was Jeanne's neighbor. I lived right over there, the fifth house on the right.

When her husband died, I offered to help her mow her lawn. I was married with children, and she had a little girl. I would address her in the formal form, *vous*. Nothing happened for ten years.

One day, I declared my love. And it happened. I left my house.

Even after we had slept in the same bed for a month, I was still calling her Madame Dufeutrel.

She died two months ago. She was the love of my life.

In the morning, we would listen to the radio and dance together in the kitchen.

I go to the cemetery every day to talk to her.

*Gérard Bruchet, 69, retired fisherman*

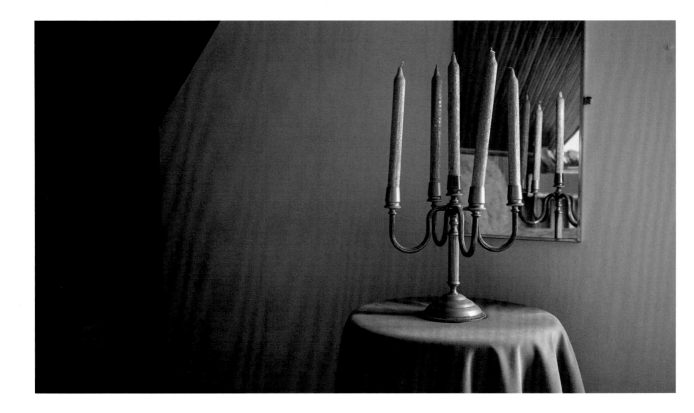

RADIO

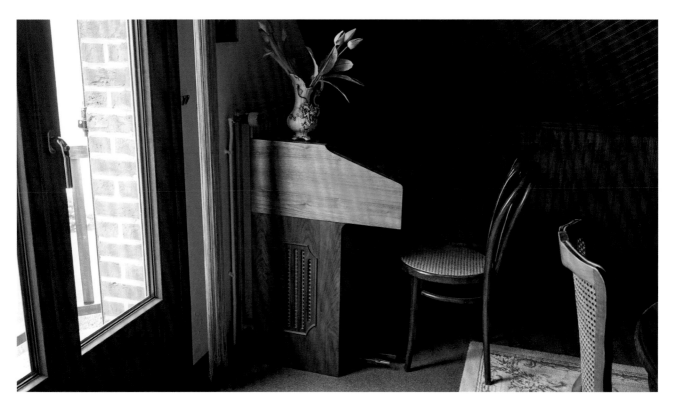

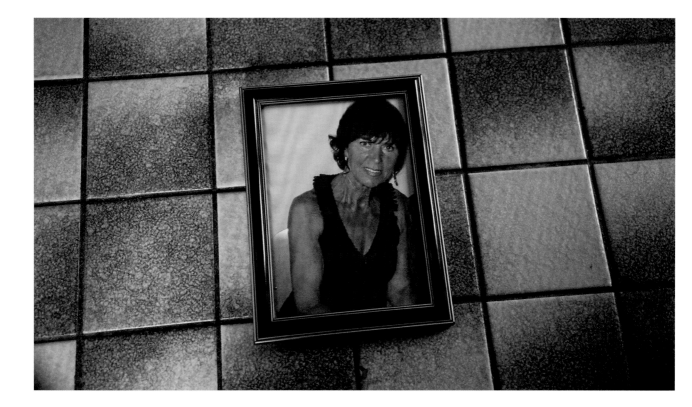

RADIO

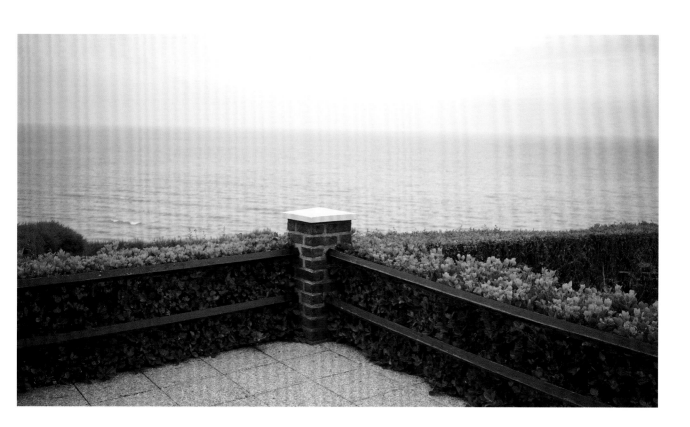

# GENTLENESS

*Le Diamant, Martinique*

I remember when I fell in love at fourteen. I remember when I fell in love at twenty. But I don't remember when I fell in love with Patrick, because it wasn't love at first sight. It wasn't passionate or intense. It just happened, in great gentleness. The encounter, the approach, the seduction. It had to simmer before it was time for love.

We were opposites. He was Catholic. I was anticlerical. He was strict. I was laidback. I loved traveling. He hated it. But we had a common passion: music. And a common dream: to start a family. So we went for it. Nine months later, our first daughter was born.

It's been twenty-three years now. We love nature. And we love having guests at home. When we go to bed at night, we are always excited to talk about our day. But we are never alone otherwise. We never organize moments to be just the two of us. I'd love to go away with him, but he doesn't want to leave the house.

I am not very interested in sex, and he asked me if he could see other women. I had to give him my permission; I understood. I would cope with the jealousy, even if that meant I had to suffer.

Not long ago, a friend of a friend stayed with us. Patrick started having feelings for her. She had feelings for him too. When she left, he told me they had kissed. I decided to write her a letter. I told her I was ready to give her my spot if she wanted it.

But it never happened. Both of them backed out.

I don't think he's found anyone yet. He is too shy.

It hasn't been easy. We fight a lot. So many times I have made lists of reasons to leave him. But I don't. Because I realize I can't live without him. I would miss him too much. We would both be so lonely if we were on our own. And I have always had this dream of staying with one person, all my life.

He says he will never leave me. I think he loves having a family too. He didn't get much love growing up, and I like making up for it. I am his wife but also his mother. And I really can feel his

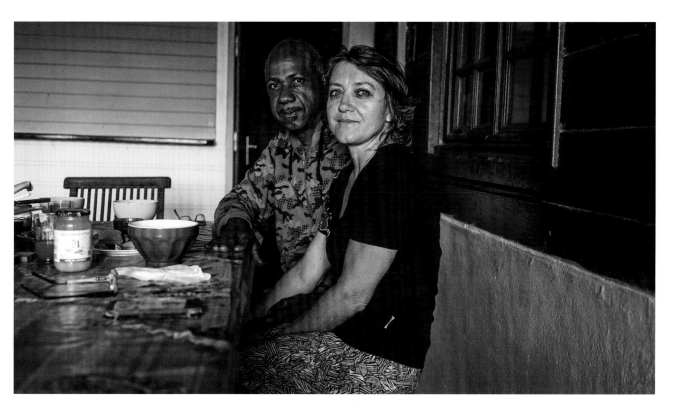

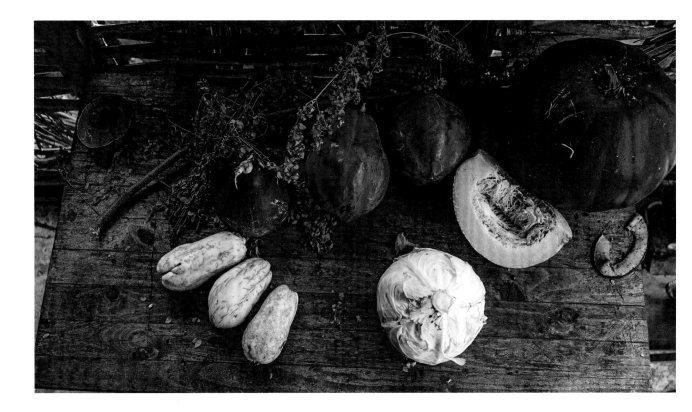

GENTLENESS

love. Sometimes he gets scared and talks to me about the day he will die. He tells me how afraid he is that I might replace him.

But I probably wouldn't.

So maybe that is love: being different and wallowing in conflict. Why would I still be here otherwise? Maybe I should be the one who needs to help him go.

*Claire Fenoy, 48, elementary school teacher*

When I was a young man, folks in the neighborhood were always asking me: "Patrick, where is your girlfriend?" But I wasn't into girls. I was interested in playing soccer, music, and putting food on the table. I had nine brothers and sisters, so I would always go down to the river to catch some crayfish for supper. Or walk four and a half miles to work on our piece of land.

But then, I turned thirty. I was still living with my parents. My brothers and sisters had all left and had babies. It was time. I was looking for a wife. One day, I was selling fish with a friend on the side of the road. And there she was: a beautiful blonde woman. It was the right moment.

It's been twenty-three years. She is open-minded. She loves people. She is a teacher. I play my music and cultivate our garden. I sell our fruits and vegetables. Our chickens give us fourteen eggs a day.

I love her. But not every day. It doesn't hold me as it used to. I always thought I was going to be the type of man that would be faithful to his wife forever. But she doesn't want to be touched anymore.

So I love her less. I really want to have sex. But not just that; I want to be in love again. I want to have those feelings again. I want to meet someone else.

But I don't want to let go of Claire because I love her anyway, despite the routine. We built a life together. We love our home. We love our house. We love our friends. We always pushed each other forward. And I can feel her love.

But if I want to make her happy, I need to be happy first. And when I asked Claire if I could see other women, she accepted.

Is Claire the woman of my life? I don't know.

Maybe there is another woman out there waiting for me.

Who knows?

I am still here.

A couple of days ago, I was working in the garden with Claire. After a moment, she had to do something in the house. "I love you," she said, leaving. "Me too," I answered.

*Patrick Muller, 53, musician and farmer*

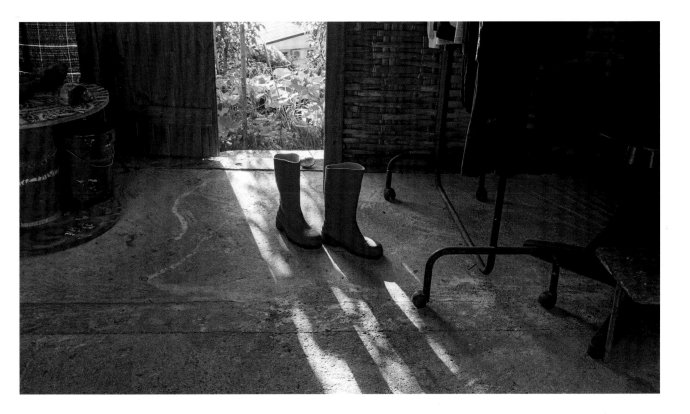

# Hair

*Nuzéjouls, Lot*

In my family, women came second. My father would always say, "If you don't behave, we'll sell you to buy candies for your brother." It stayed with me. I always thought no one would want to be with me, that no one would love me.

But I met him. I was seventeen. He was nineteen. I was so shy. One night, we finally kissed. We got married and opened a guesthouse.

He traveled a lot, and I was too afraid to tell him that running our business overwhelmed me—that I was lost and tired. I wanted his love so much that I totally erased myself.

I would do anything to make him happy. I would ask him for permission to do everything—to cut my hair, for instance. He would always tell me to stop asking. I couldn't. Whenever I would hear him come home, even if I was resting, I would get up and start doing something for him. So that he would love me. So that he wouldn't abandon me. He did though. He left me to be with another woman.

He remains the person who has given me the most love in my life; and he still does. He helps me a lot with my new house. I kept his last name.

I am grateful that he left me, because I had to learn to exist on my own. I had to learn how to say no. Today, I am capable of so many things.

I am taking care of myself now.

*Sabine Arabian, 58, guesthouse owner*

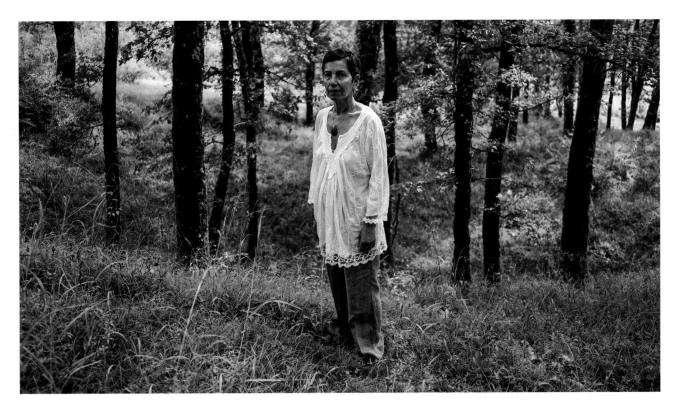

# TRUNK

I always have been very well behaved and really good at school. I was an only child. I was a loner and concentrated on my studies. No boys, no friends. Just my studies.

I went to the village fair. There, I saw a man leaning at the bar, drinking a beer. He was classy; he was beautiful; he had style. We talked for hours. I wanted to see him again. I found out where he lived and went to see him. We fell madly in love. I was seventeen. He was fifty-five.

The problem when you are seventeen and you fall in love with an older man is that you ask yourself: "Do I have a psychological problem? Do I have an Oedipus complex?" I had no experience. He was my first love.

Months became years.

We kept our relationship secret. When I was off at university and he came to pick me up at the train station, I would hide in the trunk of his car so that no one could see us. Until one day, I was walking hand in hand with Jean-Pierre in a nearby town, and I bumped into my father. My father said: "It's easy. It's either him or me. If it's him, you pack your bags, and I don't want to see you anymore." I moved in with Jean-Pierre. I didn't see my father for seven years.

I am younger than Jean-Pierre's kids, but they've always accepted me.

At twenty-five, I started feeling unwell. Breast cancer. Breast removal. Chemo. It's metastatic cancer, meaning the cancer will always be there. It will never heal.

I started receiving treatment.

We opened a restaurant.

Two years later, my bones were hurting. And there it was: bone cancer. I started another round of treatment. Ever since I turned twenty-seven, there have been ups and downs. I've undergone intense chemo, and I am in a trial program today.

Last year, I almost died, and I told Jean-Pierre, "If I survive, let's get married." I did survive. We got married in an old washhouse.

I could die at any time. But there is this

phrase that I've told myself ever since I got sick: "I have lived it"—I have lived that *love.* That emotion with the person you love, that butterfly feeling in your stomach, that beating heart, that feeling of going to pieces or of being so strong. If you don't feel that, what is life worth living for?

*Julie Lafourcade, 31, and Jean-Pierre Nouailles, 70,*
*owners of the restaurant Le Fromage Rit*

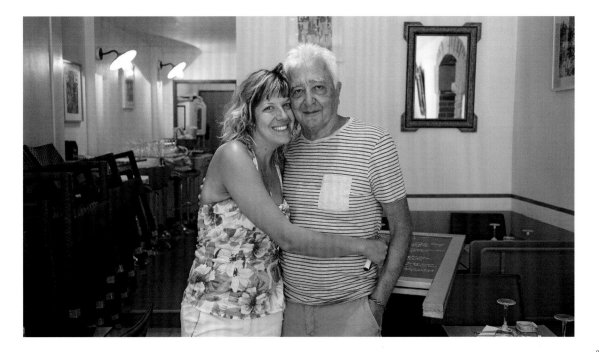

# CLOUD

*Morbier, Jura*

My wife, Nadine, died a year ago. She had lung cancer. I was with her at the hospital when she passed away. I was holding her wrist. At 5:00 a.m., she exhaled deeply, and it was over. We had been together for thirty-five years. That's not a long time; I would say it was too short.

Before she died, she told the whole family: "Jean-Patrice can't be on his own. He needs to find another woman. Don't be angry with him for that." But I tried to destroy myself. Since she couldn't come back, I thought I should join her and had suicidal thoughts.

Two months after her death, I saw this cloud in the sky. It was shaped like her. It was her. She was lying on her back with her hands on her stomach.

We talked for four days, until the cloud disappeared. She said: "Don't worry about me; I am going to be okay. You go take care of yourself." So I survived.

I went on a dating website, and I met four women. I'm with one of them now, but she is very mean to me. She tells me that I love her too much. When I have feelings, I have to share them, but then I get blamed for it. I'm so confused, I don't know what to do.

I have a weak character, and she has a strong one. She makes me feel so little sometimes. I stayed at her house twice one week, but she was so dismissive, I just couldn't bring myself to make love to her.

I'm seeing her next week. I really hope we can work things out.

*Jean-Patrice Pottier, 61, retired IT technician*

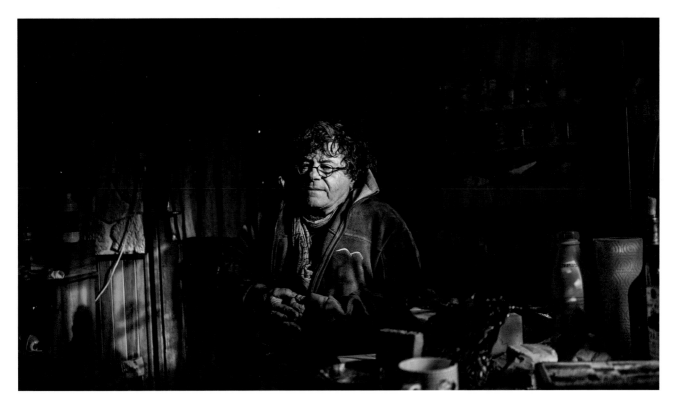

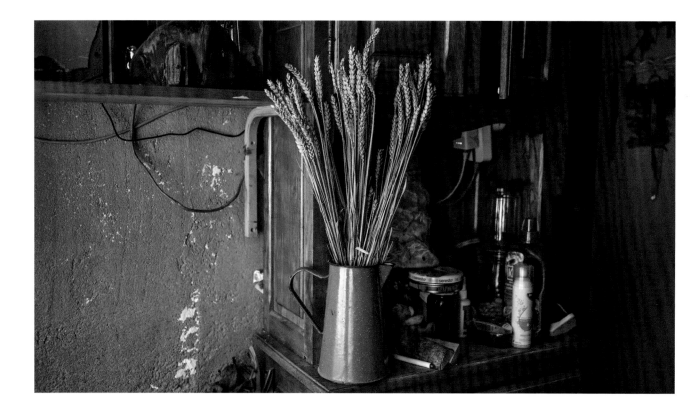

CLOUD

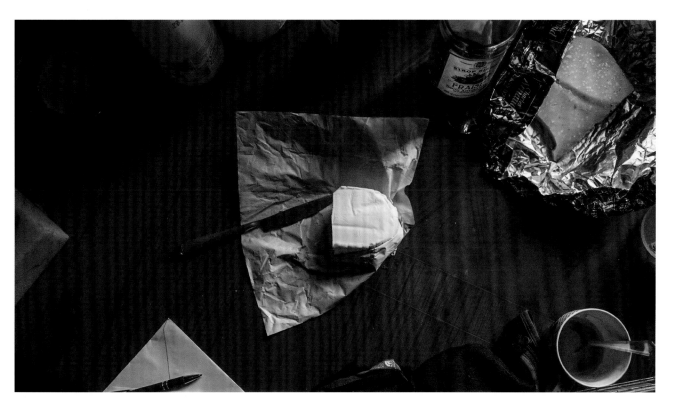

# DOG

*Pic d'Ansabère, Pyrénées-Atlantiques*

I named my cabin the Villa of Those Deprived of Love because I was the least favorite child in my family. It used to be that in farmers' families, there were maybe six children. They would send the one they loved the least into the mountains to herd sheep. And that was my case. They had very obvious preferences—especially Mom. But moms do what they can.

How do you survive that? First, I had a terrible adolescence. It was endless. I was in pain.

I was shy. The mountains were not a place for teenagers. I would come back to the village once a week, get some bread, and go back to the herd with my donkey. I would miss everything: the balls, all the activities.

But then I adapted. And I was happy. I have dedicated my whole life to the sheep. And I don't regret it at all.

I don't like humans. They are twisted. When I see what they are capable of, I am ashamed.

I would have rather been a dog. That is why I work with animals. And I love waking up every morning.

I am with Katia now. She is from Paris. She is a good person. I met her when she was seventeen and I was twenty-five. She was my employee. She loved me, but it wasn't reciprocal. I was with someone else at the time. And we spent thirty years without seeing each other. But we met again, and we got married ten years ago. I never married any of the others. Why? Because they didn't ask.

She just had an operation, so she's in Paris, resting. Do I love her? I don't know. *Love* is a weird word. I care about Katia. That must be love. She cares about me too—a bit too much.

She's the one I should have kept when I was young, because we could have done things together. But I was too stupid at twenty-five. We could have had babies together. One of them could have taken over, and I could have retired. But I am going to have to sell my flock. I haven't found anyone to replace me.

I don't want to leave.

*Marcel Etcheberry, 63, shepherd*

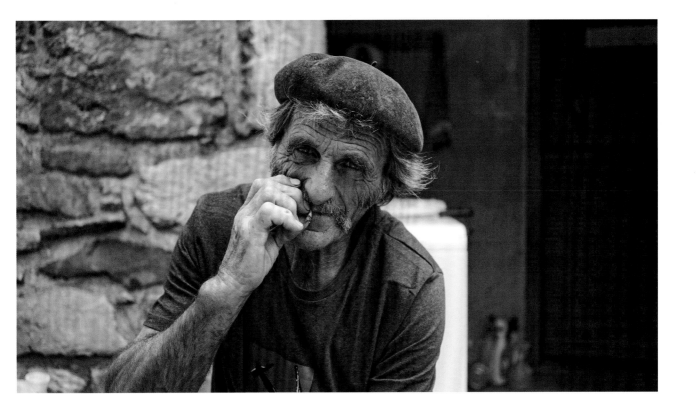

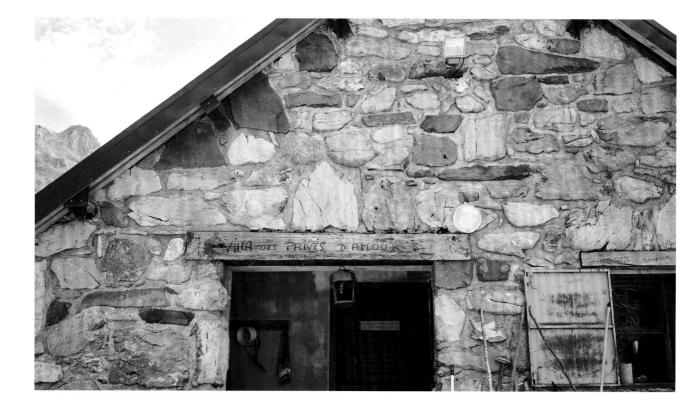

DOG

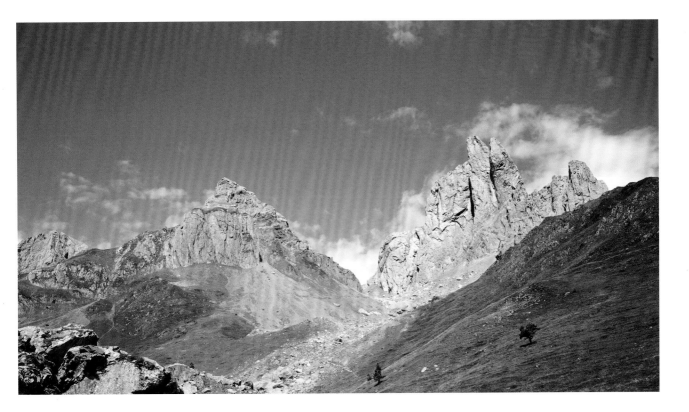

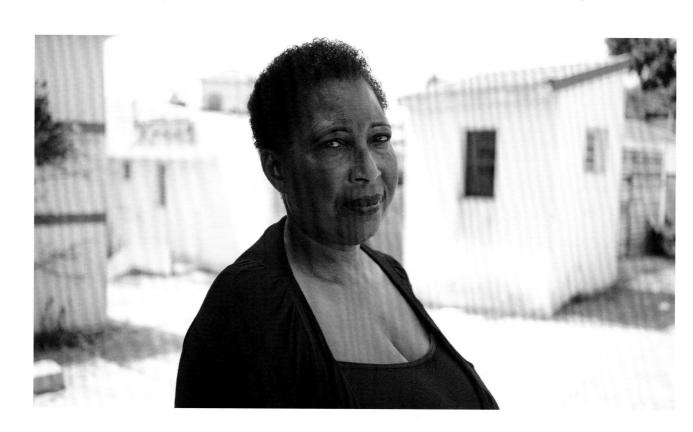

# LEMONGRASS

*Marigot, Saint Martin*

I met my husband when I was sixteen years old. He was my first boyfriend. We had four children.

But then he vanished. Disappeared. I was too poor to take care of my children, so my family took them to live in mainland France and in the United States.

Today, I live alone with my mother.

I have nothing.

No friends.

No boyfriend.

I would like to watch TV, but I don't have enough money to pay for cable. Often, I don't have money to eat. I sometimes put a branch of lemongrass and a few leaves of basil in a pot to boil, and that's all I have for the day.

I used to work as a cleaning lady, but Hurricane Irma destroyed the hotel where I worked. I am sixty years old. Nobody wants to hire me.

I would love to be with a man, but I don't want a fling. I would want us to live together, and he would need to help me financially.

I have met some men that liked me, but I didn't trust them. "What if they left me? What if they were lying?" Some women would just go for it, have a good time, go to the beach with them, and that's it. But for me, that is not a serious attitude. I would rather go to church and pray.

I really want a man, but I would rather have a job.

*Clara Michel, 60, unemployed*

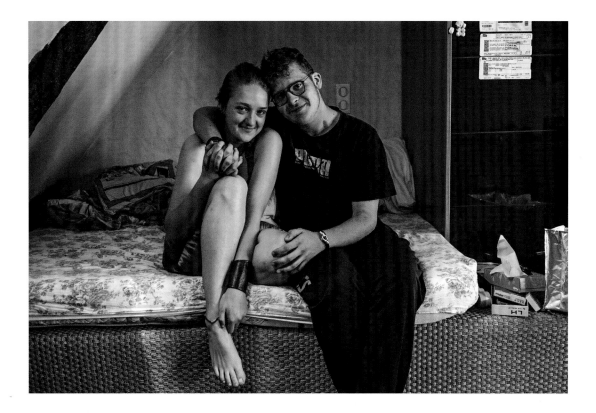

# SUGAR

*Montluçon, Allier*

Last Monday, I had to make the most difficult decision of my life. I broke up with my girlfriend. We met on a dating app, and we spent hours talking on the phone and chatting online. We never met, but I was so in love with her. She started her job as a butcher and I had to go to school, so we didn't have time to talk anymore. I called her: "Baby, we need to stop this." I cried so much. It was my week of cramming for the baccalaureate exams, and I was supposed to learn my history dates, like of the ones from the First World War. But I was too sad.

On Tuesday, my sister introduced me to Antoine. She owed me a boyfriend since she dated one of my friends. I've never questioned my sexuality. For me, it has always been a boy, a girl, a boy. And when I saw him from far away, I thought he was so ugly. He was wearing a cap, and I hate caps. But then, the closer I got, the more I thought he wasn't that bad. We spent all day together. I went home, and my mother was furious. I still hadn't worked on memorizing my history dates. I felt like crap. But my sister came to see me: "Tonight, we're sneaking out!" We crawled out the window and went to the park where Antoine was waiting. We talked till two in the morning.

On Wednesday, we were back at the park. And we kissed. The best kiss I ever had. I was chewing on a mint gum, so our tongues tasted like sugar. I knew love at first sight existed, because it happened to my sister. This was it. It was my turn.

On Saturday, I had my first experience of foreplay. I had never shown my body. I felt alive. I forgot all about my ex-girlfriend.

Sunday was my birthday, and my whole family came over. My grandmother was the first one to talk to Antoine: "Hi, I'm Nadège!"

Monday was baccalaureate time. I kept thinking about him. "What is going on?"

On Tuesday, Antoine asked me to tell him again and again that I loved him. *Je t'aime, je t'aime.* The more I told him, the more I loved him.

Last night, I made love for the first time.

*Elise Miquel, 19, pastry student*

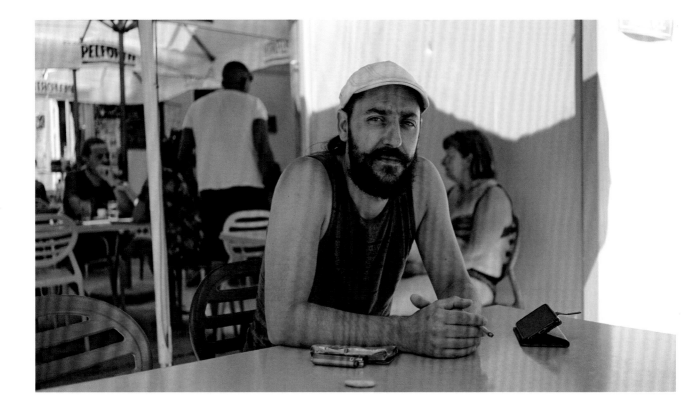

# READY

*Oraison, Alpes-de-Haute-Provence*

I have just left the woman I loved.

We met when I was twenty-eight. She was twenty-one. We both worked as trip organizers for disabled people. She really liked me. I liked her too. But I was her first lover, so I pushed back because I wanted her to meet other men. Have other experiences. See different ways of thinking. So that she could return with more wisdom.

That was my biggest mistake. Because I lost her forever. I never realized it until now.

After we met, she went back to the north of France where she lived. I returned home to the south. And for eight years, we would see each other during those work trips; sometimes on weekends. Each time, it was wonderful. We would make love and spend time together. She was joyous. Naive. I adored her facial expressions when she didn't understand the meaning of a word.

I loved her.

I would tell her all the time.

But neither she nor I made an effort to stay together. When we were apart, I had girlfriends, she had boyfriends. I was her confidant. I knew everything about them. But they came from a world I didn't belong to; they were racists and fascists. I just didn't understand how she could be with these types of men.

She had a bourgeois background. My parents were revolutionaries selling jewelry at markets. I wanted to expand her world. I wanted her to get out of her routine, go explore the unknown. I wanted to prove to her that she could do things she thought she wasn't capable of.

Last November, after eight years, I said: "Let's move in together. This is it. I am ready."

But she still wasn't.

I think this whole relationship was all in my head.

I tried as much as I could, but I kept hitting a wall.

The last time I saw her, I asked her: "How many times have I told you I loved you?"

"I can't even count," she answered.

"How many times have you told me you loved me?"

"Never," she said.

*Yannick Saulnier, 36, driver for disabled people*

# PRICE

*Thieulloy-l'Abbaye, Somme*

My parents are jealous of my relationship. They are very mean to me.

They can't stand my happiness. They bring me down constantly.

When I am single, my father is nice with me, but when I am with someone, he is very tough with me and with my partner.

It has complicated all my relationships. I used to have many clients as a beautician in the village, but my mother started bad-mouthing me so they stopped coming to me.

My new partner, Richard, helped me cut my parents out of my life. If it's the price to pay to be happy, so be it.

Richard's presence calms me down. I tell him every day that I am worn out by life.

I cry a lot. But he helps me to be strong. If I were on my own, I would kill myself.

*Anne-Sophie Mathon, 47, beautician*

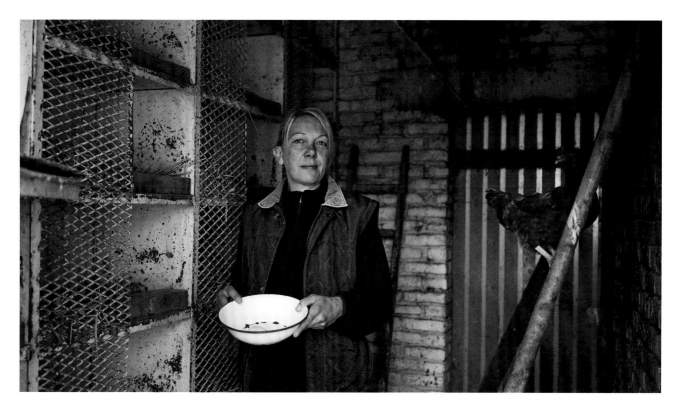

# RISE

*Capesterre-Belle-Eau, Guadeloupe*

This society we live in is full of taboos. It's closed off. Love has to be a prince and a princess. A house and kids.

But sex and flesh? They are not allowed here. And even more so if you are a woman. Because you are a slut. But never the men.

My ex-husband was my friend. He was my best friend. But I needed my freedom. I had many other partners. Men and women. And I loved each one of them. Intensely. My husband knew; I would give him all the details when I came home. That was our life, and that's how we loved each other.

But I fell in love with another man. A man I became really dependent on. I would do everything he wanted. And he made me suffer. So much. He was an alcoholic. But he was so smart. When he breathed, I breathed. That's when it hit me: Love was a disease. And emotions and sentimentality were infections.

I am single today, and I have been struggling with my thoughts. The pressure of the norm is so powerful. And after so many years, I want to know what it is just to be two. United. One. I've never had that experience. People say they "fall" in love. That word is so negative. You know what I want to do? I want to "rise" into love. That's exactly what I want to do. I want to rise and fly.

*Ketty Amacin, 57, beautician*

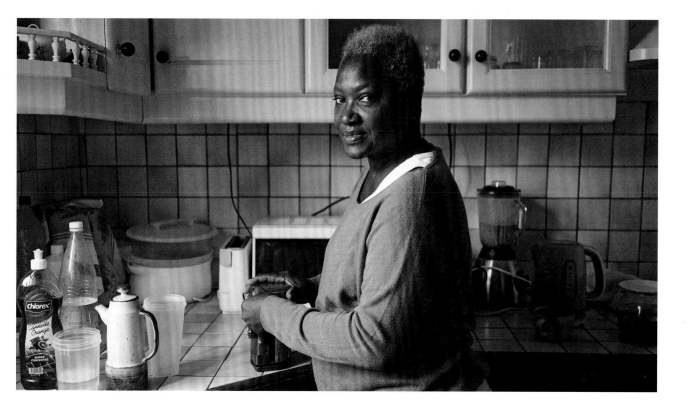

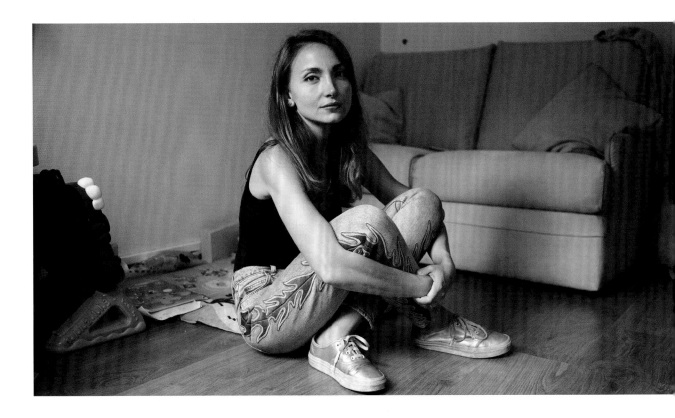

# LETTERS

*Le Chesnay, Yvelines*

I moved from Syria to France to become a biological pharmacist and a jazz singer. I was working in a lab, and this guy asked me to open the door. I will always remember how he was dressed: gray jeans, a camel leather jacket, a beautiful bag that he had bought in Poland—very stylish, very minimalist—and sneakers.

For a year, I wasn't interested, and then it just hit me. I would walk through the halls hoping to bump into him, and I finally asked him out.

I remember our first kiss. I was sleeping at the International House, and he dropped me off on his scooter. I kissed him quickly on the lips and ran away. I was thinking: "I did it!" He told me he drove so fast after that. Six months later, we moved in together.

Nicolas was a brilliant man, very intelligent, too intelligent. He pushed me to sing. He would always tell me things I had forgotten about myself.

He loved to organize special moments for his friends. He had a van because he was a surfer.

One day, he decided to organize a cheese fondue dinner party in the van!

Nicolas got diagnosed with cancer on June 21, 2014.

He wanted a child. I didn't want one. It was a difficult decision, but I came to realize that if anything were to happen to him, at least I would have a memory of him in our child.

It's the best thing we could have done. Sara was his ray of light. I am so happy he experienced being a father.

He wrote me letters.

He also wrote letters for Sara. He tells her about his story, his dreams. Profound thoughts about the meaning of life. They encourage her never to be afraid. And he writes that to love is the most important thing.

Nicolas died on April 11, 2017.

Thanks to him, I am not afraid of anything.

He was my candle.

He was my guide.

*Lynn Adib, 31, biological pharmacist and singer-musician, and Nicolas Zwierz (June 24, 1981–April 11, 2017)*

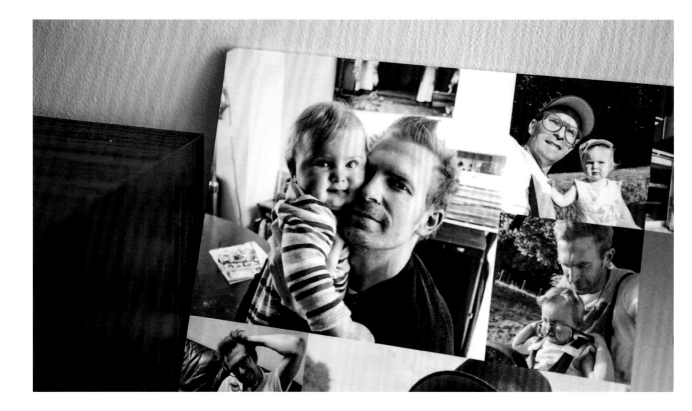

25/10/2015

Sara ma petite puce adorée
je suis ton papa je m'appelle
. Nicolas et ma vie se résume
à cela :
- j'ai passé 4 ans en Pologne (de
4 ans (à 8 ans). C'était les plus belles
années de ma vie. J'ai passé ces
années dans la nature : dans la forêt,
à la plage, dans la neige. Nous
avions un très grand chien qui
s'appelait TILA. J'aimais beaucoup
ma petite sœur Caroline mais j'ai
toujours eu un mauvais caractère
alors je me disputais beaucoup avec
elle même si je l'aimais énormément.
Mes amis : mes véritables amis à
Swinaysué était RITA et KOLESZ (qui
était mon copain en polonais) Avec les
...vaient 50 ans de
...meilleurs

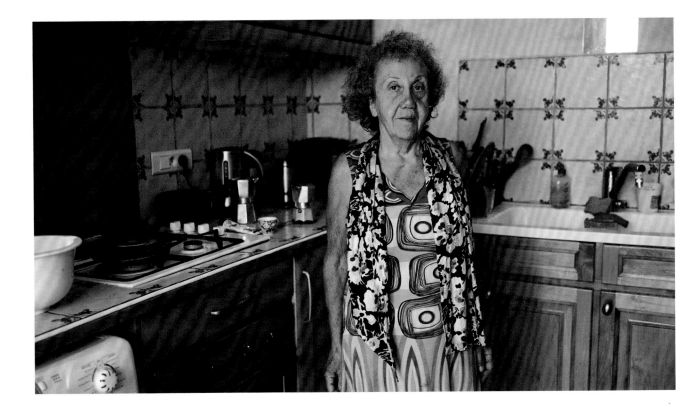

# HAT

*Die, Drôme*

We were both committed to the single life.

Until we met.

I was forty-nine and he was forty-one. When I first saw him, I saw his soul. He was rebellious and angry; I liked that.

But it was work. I always assumed my partners thought like I did. That never happens. He and I couldn't even spend more than four hours together at the beginning. We had been living by ourselves for so long, we were not used to making any compromises. But I was very lonely, and all I wanted was to have a routine with someone.

Then it happened: we actually stayed together for one whole night. When we woke up, he turned to me and said: "There was no crying and no yelling, hurray!" And we laughed. And laughed some more. And more. We got married. He was wearing a yellow sweater, and I was wearing a red dress.

It's been twenty-one years. I love to smell him. I would say he smells like spicy musk.

When he was a little boy, he was placed in an orphanage because his parents couldn't care for him. I was too old to have children, so we decided to adopt a child. His name is Herizo. That means "strong and honest" in Malagasy. He was eight years old when he arrived. I remember him putting his hat on top of ours on the buffet table during our first winter together. A way to seal our burgeoning relationship.

To this day, every morning, when my husband and I wake up, it's as if we hadn't seen each other for ten years. We take each other in one another's arms as if we are meeting again after a long, long time.

*Linette Guéron-El Houssine, 69, writer*

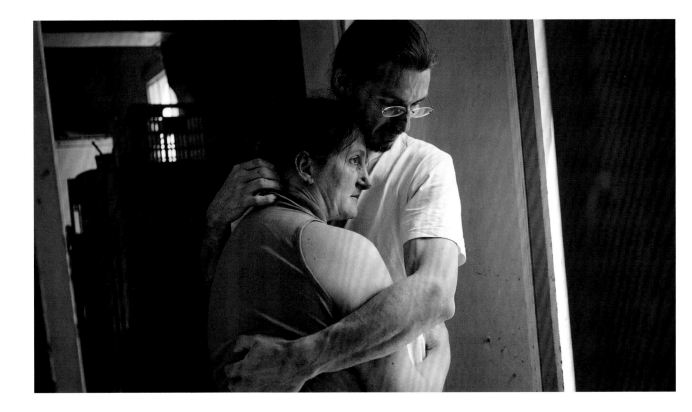

# BREAD

*Le Mesnil-Germain, Calvados*

I have the impression that we are not educated to have feelings. I was a very cheerful child, but adults took it away from me. I was very sensitive, so I closed myself off to stop suffering or feeling any emotion. It allowed me to stay among others while remaining hidden.

Today, I am still very reserved, but I am learning to feel again. I am cracking my armor. Living in nature has helped me do that. Sitting in the grass and experiencing rushes of joy. It's a constant journey of self-seeking: "Who am I?"

Lucile and I have been together for twenty-four years. My guiding principle in life has been building a life with her, then with her and our children. Not building a professional career. There is something sacred. We don't have to talk to understand each other. We often burst into laughter because I say a word, then she says another, and we are thinking the same thing.

When you lose faith in who you are and who you want to be, the other reminds you of what they see in you. And that's vital. Like an anchor. We could get lost if we weren't two.

Every night, she and my daughter fall asleep together in our bed after reading a story.

And when I am finished making bread, I go into the room, take my daughter in my arms and tuck her back into her bed.

*Nicolas Bernouis, 41, baker and farmer,*
*and Lucile Bernouis, 42, cheesemaker and farmer*

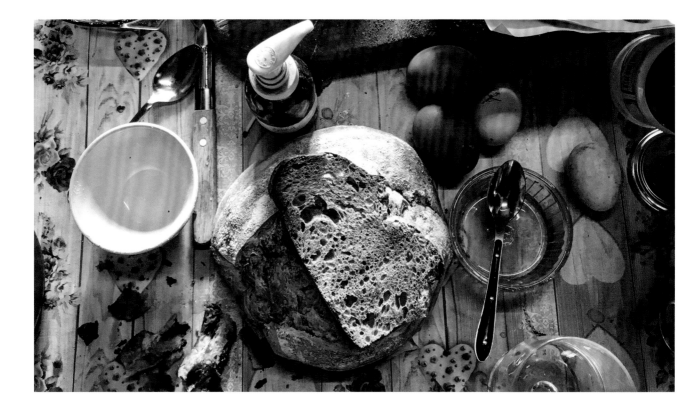

Bread

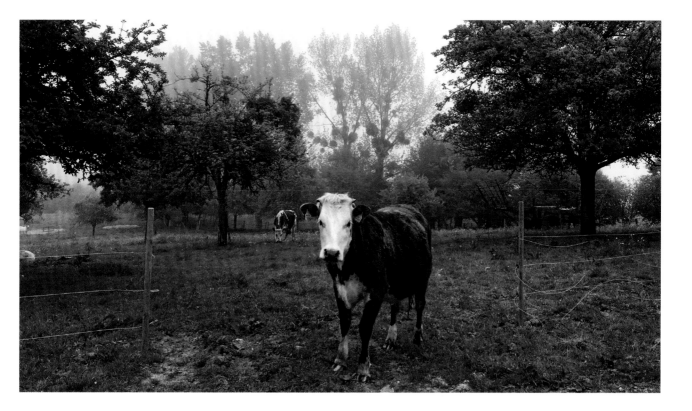

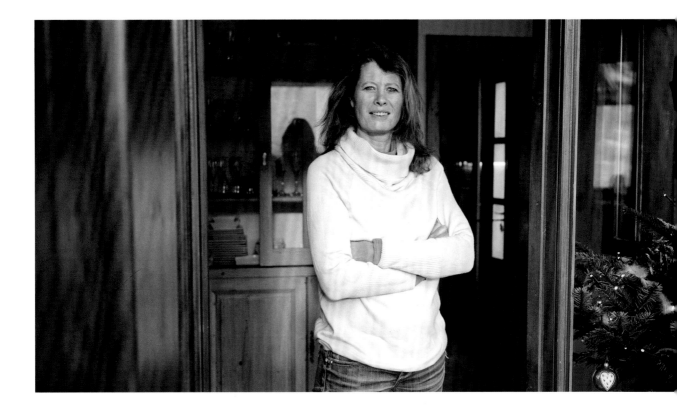

# END

*Domancy, Haute-Savoie*

I was married for eighteen years, and we had three children together. But we were suffering too much. There was no more love or communication. I had become more of a mom than a lover. I felt imprisoned. So we divorced. I was heartbroken.

Today, I am with a man. I met him at work. He made me laugh, and I played along. He fell head over heels. And so did I.

It was so passionate when we were together that he would cry when he had to leave.

But it's very complicated. He's married, and we have been together for one year. His wife knows he is seeing me. I told him not to leave her.

What am I searching for? Love, for sure. But I am always looking for that one relationship that will heal my wounds. And I am always looking for that one relationship that I know will end. My father left when I was eleven, so I am always going to be looking for the person who is going to abandon me.

I have always been in love with men much older than me—except my husband. The others have been ten, fifteen years older. The one I am with now is twenty years older.

So you see, I am preparing to be abandoned. To repeat the pattern.

But I love him. I love him profoundly.

*Delphine Lacquement, 50, human resources manager and laughter yoga teacher*

# SOUL MATE

*Perpignan, Pyrénées-Orientales*

"Salomé, I want to fall in love with you." It was her that I wanted, no one else. So I told her. We have been together for nine years and have a four-year-old boy.

I have found fulfillment only as part of a couple. Never in friendship. A woman is going to give you her word. A man can let you down. But maybe I have never had the right friends.

Salomé disrupted my life entirely. At the beginning of our relationship, she asked me if I was attracted to other women. I said yes. It seemed unimaginable to me that I could say that. In my previous relationships, anything could look like a betrayal. There was no room for dialogue. But no, not with Salomé.

Everything changed the day a woman came into our lives. We formed a threesome. We were happy. It seemed very natural to be the three of us. That completely changed my vision of love. Before, I was like everyone else, in exclusive relationships and invariably anguished. But from then on, making love to another person was no longer a reason for breaking up. Man or woman. With or without Salomé.

But it's not just about sex. It's about feelings. It can't be fleeting. I need to be in love. It doesn't mean I'm going to leave Salomé. Besides, as soon as I meet a woman, I always want to introduce them. Because there will always and only be Salomé. She is my soul mate. She is my friend. She is my only friend, actually. And I told her: "Salomé, you are the last chance I am giving to love." Because no one else will ever know me as well as she does.

Together, we will have challenged everything. I think I have reached a total point of fusion with her. But I don't know if the same goes for her. And it makes me anxious. I want her to fall in love with other people, to have her life shaken, to explore her feelings. But it worries Salomé; she doesn't want to let go. She doesn't want to fall in love with another person.

But I will be here. I am not going anywhere.

*Jean-Loup Carrénard, 37, and Salomé Blechmans, 32, filmmakers, and their son, Avishaï, 4*

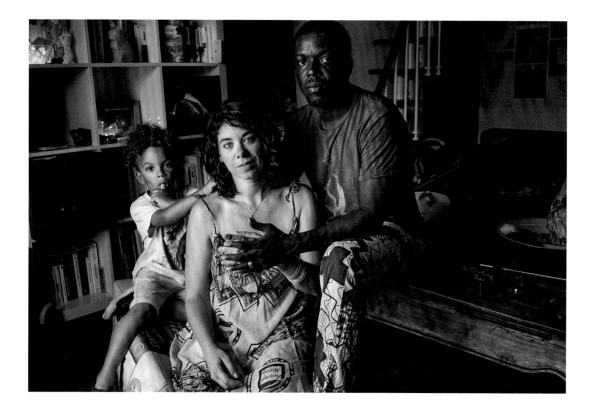

# Will-o'-the-Wisp

*Marle, Aisne*

My husband had left me, so I looked for a job and started working as a cook in a medical institute. That's where I met Michel. He was an electrician there. It did not start well. It started with a fight.

There was a stray cat at the institute that had kittens. I wanted to adopt one, but he wouldn't let me. And I thought: "What an idiot!" But Michel was always looking at me. Finally, we patched things up—well, in our own way.

We didn't fall in love right away. But does love at first sight really exist?

My ex-husband had left me for another woman. I couldn't have kids, so we had adopted a girl together. She was three months old when she arrived. I didn't care that he cheated on me; what made me angry was that he cheated on his daughter. You don't fight for ten years to have a child and then just say: "I'm out!" He no longer sees her.

Men were all the same for me. But with Michel, I started trusting them again.

The first time we slept together, it was like there were four of us in the bed. It was really tough.

Michel had been married for fourteen years. Me too. And for some reason, even though my husband had left me, I felt like I was cheating on him. It wasn't easy.

Still, we moved in together very quickly. For the kids. I had my girl; he had three kids. They were my family right from the start.

Love came. He is a good man. We do everything together: the dishes, the cleaning. I am not the type of woman who has to show everyone that we love each other. But Michel, he does. I love him. He loves me madly, sometimes almost to the point of suffocation.

We have been together for twenty-nine years. Even if it hadn't worked out with Michel, I think I would have sacrificed myself and stayed with him. For the kids. A child has the right to happiness. An adult can get over it.

*Liliane Pertin, 62, childcare provider*

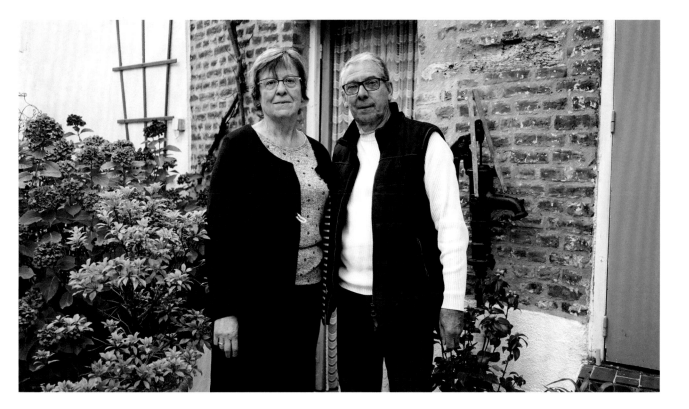

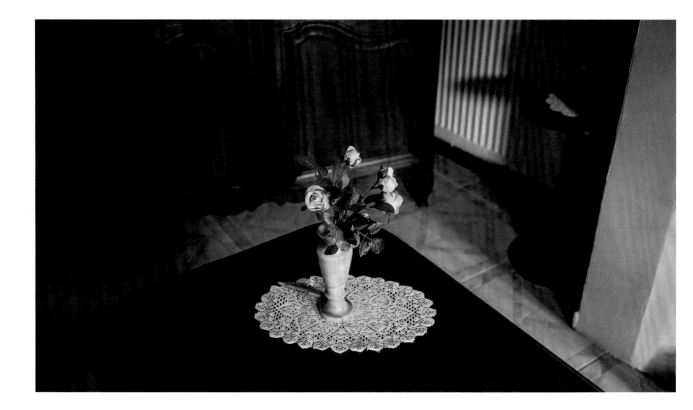

WILL-O'-THE-WISP

Almost every day, there was a power outage. It was always at lunchtime. I would go fix it because I was the handyman. And I would stop by the cafeteria because there was always leftover dessert. So every day, I would see Liliane. We would look at each other, even though we were mad at each other because of the cat episode. But we had orders: if we found cats, we had to kill them. I couldn't just give her one. Our relationship started with insults. Nevertheless, my buddies already pictured me married to her.

I was going through a divorce at that time. My ex had moved to the south. I was taking care of my three kids alone. It was really hard to manage all of it. And then I learned she had been cheating on me with several men. Because people like to talk. It really hurt me. I was ashamed; I was the cuckold. I was so embarrassed; I didn't even dare see my parents anymore. People didn't divorce at the time.

With Liliane, there was no declaration of love. Our children have always been the priority and we re-created a tight-knit family. Our love is a will-o'-the-wisp. If I got back on my feet, it is thanks to her. If I had stayed alone, I don't know where I would be today. Maybe I wouldn't be here anymore.

She can be difficult. Everything has to be perfect. Right away. Not in three days.

I am more on the relaxed side. As long as I can work in my garden.

*Michel Pertin, 70, retired electrician*

# JAW

*Le Lamentin, Martinique*

I went to a party, and he was the only person I didn't talk to. But a couple of days later, he found me on Facebook Messenger. I bombarded him with questions. Job? Kids? Money? He checked all the boxes, and I was hooked immediately. He was so affectionate.

But very quickly, he became cold and distant. Authoritarian. I wasn't allowed to leave anything at his house. Nothing. He even brought me back my washcloth once. He wouldn't introduce me as his girlfriend at parties. He never slept through the night at my house. He never ate what I cooked for him. One Christmas, I was alone, and he didn't even invite me over to celebrate with his friends.

When I tell him, he gets so angry. I do realize I have a strong character and that I am independent financially, so I have tried to be more docile.

I think love doesn't exist. Or that it's never reciprocal. The only time he says he loves me is when we get in terrible fights. Last year, we got in a big one, and he displaced my jaw. But you know what? It actually got us closer. He was so full of guilt, he took great care of me.

There is a French saying: to live happy, live hidden. He likes to say it to me. And I like that idea—that it is just the two of us. But that was not what he meant. He just wants to hide me from his other girls. I know he cheats on me. Men are not faithful; I understand that. But I am his girlfriend, and he is getting sloppy. I found a used condom in his trash yesterday.

So I broke up with him this morning. This time, I really hope he doesn't call me. Because if he does, I will forgive him again.

I love him. Deeply.

But I have to start thinking about my survival.

*Joëlle Jougon-Beauprés de Monsalès, 39, professor*

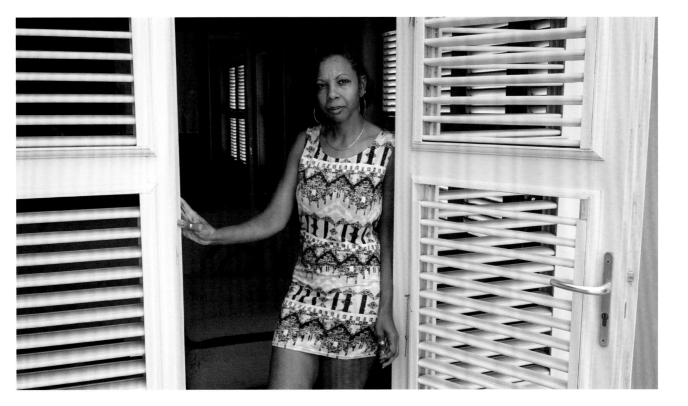

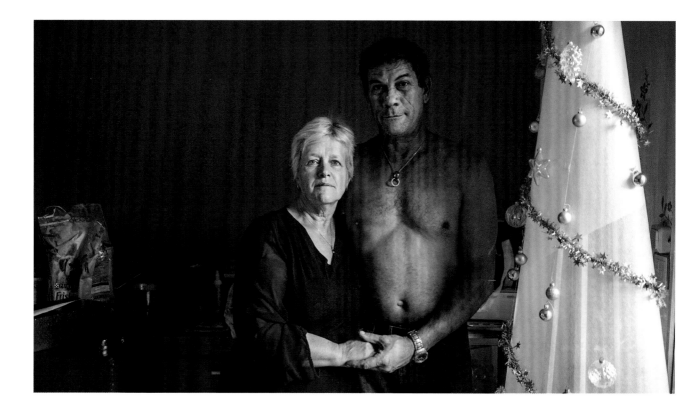

# BLAME

*Quincey, Haute-Saône*

After ten years with my ex-boyfriend, I posted on Facebook: "For our anniversary, we are giving each other a gift: we are separating." And I signed up for a dating website.

I met forty men in one year. It was a great way to go out, dress up, and feel pretty.

One day, Thierry contacted me on the site. We talked on the phone at 4:30 p.m. At 5:35 p.m., we met for coffee. I was five minutes late. As we were walking toward the bistro, he asked me: "Can I hold your hand?" The way my hand fit in his was perfect. Dry and soft.

He came to my place the next day, and he never left.

It wasn't love at first sight with Thierry. His web profile was too perfect. A lot of men had lied to me. He said he cooked; he doesn't. But he does do the cleaning.

He tells me he loves me, that he thinks I am pretty. Last time he told me was yesterday, at noon.

It's been two years. We can't live without each other.

I want to do everything for him. All his problems are mine; I need to solve them. If I walk by him three times, I'll kiss him at least once. I have never met a man who loves me like he does.

I will not blame him if it has to end. Because even if we spend only ten years together, I know it will have been intense and beautiful.

I think life is worth living because I can give love. I don't need to receive it. I had been married for twenty-four years. My ex-husband was depressed. I wanted to save him. I was so afraid to leave him because he was so sick. But I needed to go. Five years later, he committed suicide on the anniversary of our divorce.

*Chantal Lambert, 58, dog sitter,*
*and Thierry Laplanche, 60, paramedic*

# KIDNEY

*Fleury, Aude*

I met my husband when I was nineteen. He was working for my father.

We trust each other. We are complementary. He is solitary, and I am very sociable. I like French music, and he likes disco.

I call him Amour, and we fall asleep every night holding hands.

We have two children: Emma, sixteen, and Mathis, eleven.

We didn't plan on having Emma. I was totally panicked. But when she arrived, it was pure happiness.

It happened in December last year. Emma kept telling me she was tired. Her nose was bleeding all the time. One day, she was sleeping at a friend's house, and she called me to pick her up. I brought her to the emergency room. At 4:00 p.m., they told me it was kidney failure.

She was in danger. Her blood was poisoned. Her heart had doubled in size, her breathing was poor and her blood pressure was very high. She was very close to having a stroke.

They plugged her into a dialysis machine to filter her blood.

I kept crying. And I asked myself: "Why?" She had never been sick. She was an equestrian; she was always running around. It's an injustice that you just don't understand.

Then, there was the question of the kidney transplant. Our whole family and all our friends were ready to give her a kidney. We did tests. It took nine months to get the results.

Both my husband and I were compatible. We kept fighting about who would give their kidney. I had the nurse on the phone, and I asked her to do "rock-paper-scissors." She laughed and wrote my name down.

For a mother, it is symbolic: it is like giving birth to your child again.

Emma got her transplant on June 28.

She is already dancing again.

*Caroline Fabre, 43, horse riding instructor*

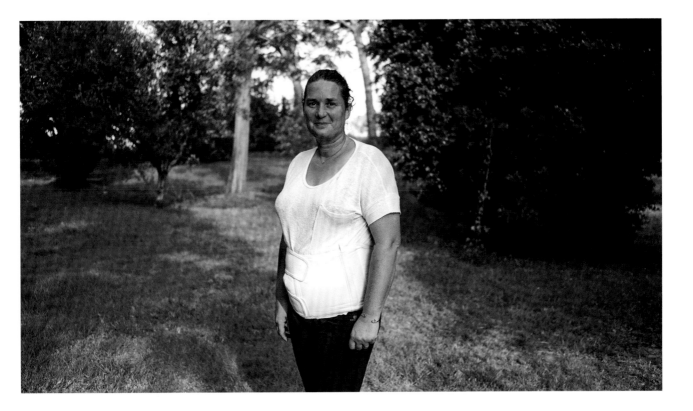

# Apples

*Châtillon-en-Diois, Drôme*

I don't like to talk about myself. I am reserved. I sell apples and wine. That's it.

I love love. I am a poet. But I have never been with a woman. I prefer platonic love. I've never tried to be with a woman, and I've never been interested in sex.

What I like is to seduce women. Give them a sunflower. Recite a poem. I do adore them. And since I cannot have them all, I prefer to charm them all.

I am not frustrated. I sleep alone. I am happy the way I am. Happiness is not necessarily being part of a couple.

But sometimes I doubt the fact that a woman could ever love me. Sometimes, I realize I was too afraid to ask. That I always have been afraid of getting my heart broken. Of being disappointed. Or losing the person.

I don't know how to say: "I love you."

*Eric Joanin, 58, apple cultivator and shopkeeper*

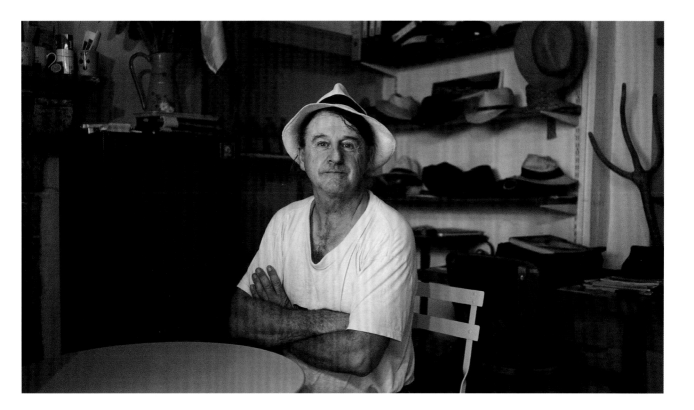

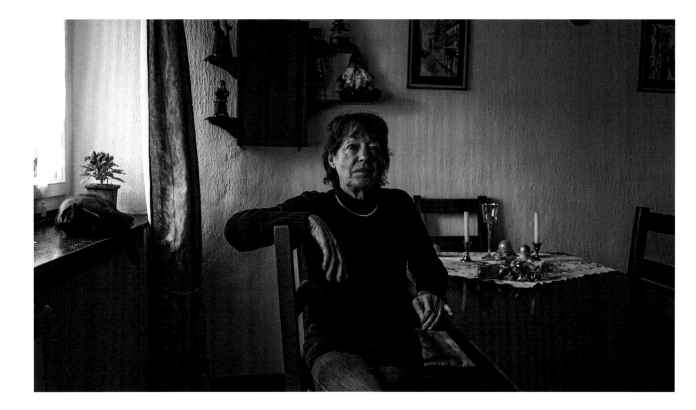

# ASHES

*Saint-Lothain, Jura*

My husband was the most important person in my life.

I was supposed to meet up with my boyfriend of the time at the Argenteuil train station. And his girlfriend was supposed to meet him. Neither came.

We looked at each other but didn't speak. He was wearing a black leather jacket. I was seventeen. He was twenty. We ended up at the same restaurant, meeting the same friends. This time, we talked. It wasn't love at first sight. In French, we say, *coup de foudre*—a lightning bolt—but after lightning, isn't there always a storm?

Today, people get married too quickly. We waited three years, and we were ready. We lived in the Paris suburbs, and on a whim, we moved to the mountains, to a village with eighty inhabitants. And six hundred cows.

He died last year of colon cancer. He didn't smoke, drink. Nothing. But he died the way he wanted; he didn't want to be old and bedridden. At the end, he couldn't talk. He was too medicated.

For me, the most incredible part of our relationship was that we helped each other grow. He was tolerant. I wasn't. When I would criticize someone, he would tell me: "But what do you know about it?" I had a good relationship with my parents, but there wasn't any affection. In his family, there was. And he gave me a lot. I would get worried when he would break his back to get wood to heat the house, but he would tell me: "Well, you do the ironing, the cleaning, and you cook!" We each had our role. We were married forty-seven years.

After he died, my dog started looking up at the ceiling a lot. I searched it on the internet, and it said it was a dog's way of mourning. Was he feeling a presence? I don't know. But I don't think my husband's spirit is still around, nor do I see any signs.

I do talk to him a lot. Each time I do something, I always wonder what he would think. I now see the world both through my eyes and through his.

The day he died, I didn't feel anything. I took pills not to cry or fall apart. I wanted to remain dignified. We dispersed his ashes in the forest. I would never ever want to visit a stone.

I don't think I'll ever get over his death. And I have no idea how you can ever get over it.

The last words he told me were: "Don't cry, Geneviève. I will always be with you."

*Geneviève Perreault, 68,*
*retired administrative assistant*

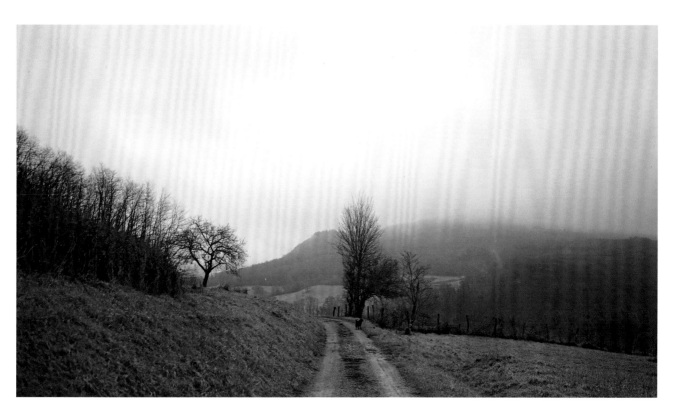

# PLANE

### Deshaies, Guadeloupe

I was working at a bar. So was she. On our third date, she kissed me on the corner of my lips. We moved in together.

But I had a problem. I was addicted to gambling. All my money went into it. So at home, it got bad. Rotten eggs. An empty fridge. We even collected points on pizza boxes.

But she got me out of it. She saved me. And because of everything she had done for me, I asked her to marry me.

A few years in, she started having flashbacks of her grandfather molesting her. And I doubted her. I wasn't there for her. She got really depressed. I suddenly had to take care of everything at home, and I started bossing her around. She was struggling. So was I. I just couldn't fill that void she had in her. But I loved her—so much.

We needed a way out. She suggested Canada.

Yes. That was the plan. But something was off. When we made love, it was brutal. "What is going on?" I asked. "I am cheating on you," she said. I hadn't gambled for three years, but that night, I gave someone fifty euros to play for me.

She said she regretted it and stayed.

The day before we left for Canada, we booked a room at the airport hotel. But she said she needed to be with him: "One last time." I begged her not to go. She still did and came back the next morning.

The plane took off. I turned to her: "Charlotte, I am leaving you." I just couldn't do it anymore. And I bought a ticket for Guadeloupe.

Here I am now.

Lost.

*Stéphane Buchs, 27, unemployed*

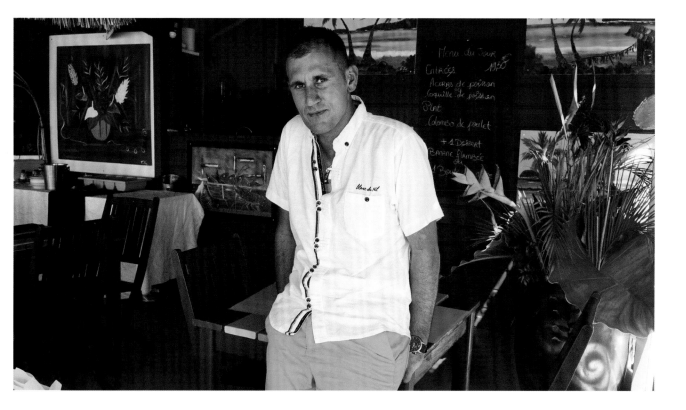

# JOURNEY

I saw my father hit my mom. I saw my father rape my mom. So, love? I had a pretty bad image of it. The men I was with were just for physical purposes—sex and then *ciao, bye-bye*. I was mean. I was distant. I was angry at my father. I was going to be independent. I would not let a man tell me what to do or to have any power over me. I could not open my heart.

Until I met her. She would call me in the morning to wake me up. Ring my doorbell and take me to the beach. One night, we kissed. I was so destabilized. What was going on? My model was a man, a house, and kids. I was falling in love with a woman. And I told her. But she had just been playing with me. She introduced me to her girlfriend.

I went back on the internet. I reached out to this woman. We decided to meet in a supermarket. I remember what she had in her shopping cart: beers, peaches, and a Spanish omelet. I was too afraid to talk to her so I walked past her, hoping she wouldn't see me. But she did. "You come back here," she said. I wish I hadn't. Because I can still feel the pain today.

She was a prostitute. But I didn't care. It was her job. When she came home, she would ask me: "Frédérique, please make love to me." She had five kids, and they became mine. I had a family now. I was an adult. I fell in love with her. I stopped working to take care of the kids. I would bring them to school, cook, pick them up, cook again.

But she changed. She had never been tender with me, but after a while, she didn't treat me well either. The days she was at home, she would play video games while I was cleaning the apartment. I got really depressed. She would never tell me she loved me; she would tell me I was crazy. But I didn't want to leave: I was too afraid of solitude, and I loved the kids. In the end, she left me for another woman.

Now, I am with a girl from Marseille. I love her. But she is married. She is never going to leave him. I know it.

I'm not happy. Who really is? I think that's the

goal in life, to always be pursuing happiness in some way. That's what keeps us alive, no? I am not sure love solves everything either. It's not enough.

Today, I don't feel lonely. Or not anymore, at least. I tried to kill myself several years ago. It didn't work; I didn't die. So I had no choice but to live.

What is it all for? I still have no answer. Maybe for all the simple moments. Seeing kids play. Flowers. Landscape. I feel that when I meet someone, I breathe new life into them, and then they leave me. Man or woman. I think I am meant to be alone. Sometimes I wonder: "Who will take care of me?" But all my lovers gave me a piece of themselves. Each of them changed me. And I can continue my journey, thanks to them.

I will be okay.

*Frédérique Leloutre, 41, human resources manager*

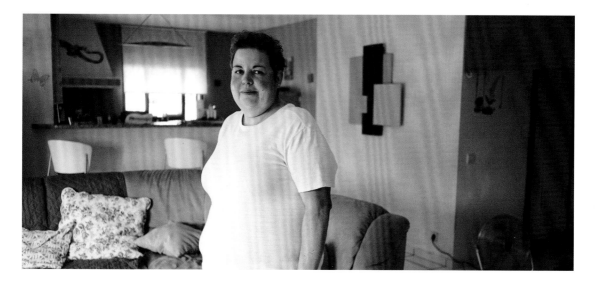

# STIMULI

*Megève, Haute-Savoie*

Love is beautiful. Love makes you blind. But love can make you very sad and destroy you.

I kissed the first woman I loved on January 14, 2005. I was twenty. I remember the date because it was her birthday. I was waiting for that one girl I had feelings for to make love, and she was the one.

But one night, I drank too much and got very jealous. I got angry and extremely violent verbally. She got scared. I wrote her a letter to apologize. She came back, but it wasn't the same.

She left me again. I was in love. I was traumatized. I was just too sad and needed answers. I totally lost my footing and had to go to a mental hospital.

A few years later, when I was twenty-six, I met this wonderful girl. A jewelry maker. One day, she went on my computer and found all these messages I was exchanging with an ex. She thought I was cheating on her. I wasn't. Even though she said she still loved me, she just couldn't trust me anymore. I tried to get her back, but it didn't work.

That same year, on my birthday, I attempted suicide. I don't tell this to everyone; it can scare people away. It wasn't her fault. I was very sensitive. My parents were divorcing. I had no self-confidence.

I have been single since then. I am thirty-three now. I don't have children. All my friends do. It's taken a toll on me. I want to build something.

Love is as vital as it is destructive. I compare it to nociception, which is the sensory nervous system's response to harmful stimuli: pain. And love can be the worst agony, worse than health problems.

I have not been working for the last two months. I drank too much at a work party and was asked to take a leave of absence. At the same time, my bosses said they loved my work, so I'm confused. I'm back on antidepressants and sleeping pills, but they don't have too much effect on me. Last night, I cried; I just felt very lonely.

I think I would do anything for love. I would never kill anyone for it. Just maybe one person: myself.

*Brice Duc-Dodon, 33, operations manager*

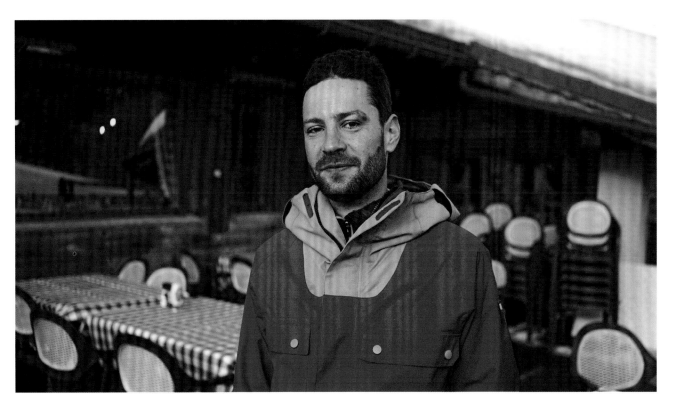

# Stars

*Miscon, Drôme*

Three years ago, I was dating four men at the same time. It was wonderful. I was beaming and fulfilled. We saw each other when we wanted to see each other. There was no jealousy and a lot of love to share. They confided in me. I confided in them. They all knew about each other. There was no ambiguity that could mess it all up.

I took a break to go see my friends who work as shepherds in the southwest of France, and there was Arnaud. He was a shepherd too. He was heartbroken. He had just left his partner of eight years, and he was fragile. We talked about love. My free spirit versus his desire to be with the one woman he loved.

A year later, he invited me to join him in the mountains. I took my backpack and walked to his pasture. We were just friends. But one night, he looked at me and said: "You are the mother of my children. I know it." We were sleeping under the stars. We held each other for a long time in the dark.

A few nights later, some of his sheep escaped. We went looking for them. It was pitch-black. And it happened. We made love in the grass.

I moved in with Arnaud. I had never felt such deep emotions. I got pregnant.

But I became jealous of the baby. I became jealous thinking of all the moments alone with Arnaud that I was going to miss out on. I was still thirsty for us. I became envious of his friends who helped him build our house. I had moved here for Arnaud, and I had no friends. I relied on him for everything. I was constantly afraid of losing him and felt imprisoned by my love for him. Daily routine was kicking in, and we were losing intensity.

Finally, Sol was born. And he brought with him a flow of love.

Today, Arnaud and I are hooked together again. We are parents now.

But I feel we still have so much to learn about each other.

I love him. Life goes on.

*Héodes Fardeau, 28, shoemaker*

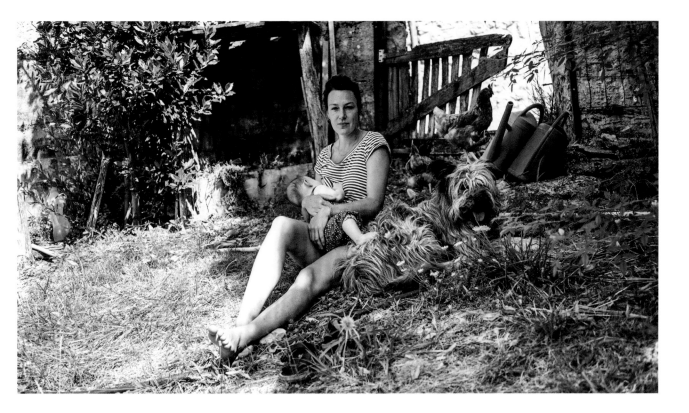

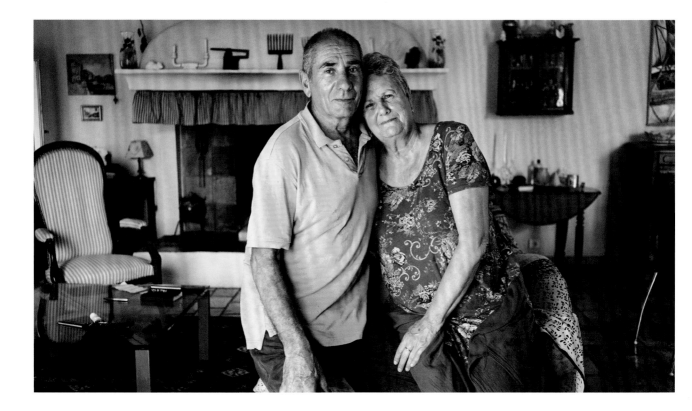

# TOENAILS

*Port-de-Bouc, Bouches-du-Rhône*

We met randomly at a street party. We had never seen each other before. We could have; we were in the same school, but the girls' building was on one side and the boys' on the other. The next day, dressed in his white pants, he drove right past my house on his moped.

Right after our first kiss, he went to boarding school, and later, he was called up for his military service. The pain of being separated was so intense; we would write each other, one, two, three letters a day. We have a cardboard box with three hundred love letters. I put it upstairs in the closet where I store our linens. Even today, if we are separated for more than five minutes, I feel that same exact pain I felt when I was seventeen.

It's been fifty years. I am old now, sixty-seven. My eyes are weak, I can't read books anymore, and I can't bend down. He will sit down, cut my toenails, and rub my legs with cream.

He is so strong. He built this house. He is replacing the shutters now. All on his own. He also dresses so well. When I look at him, my hearts thumps and I still get jealous.

Time used to be suspended. We didn't notice time passing. Today, we can count on the fingers of our hands how long we have left to live. But we are not afraid.

*Paule Grech, 67, retired florist*

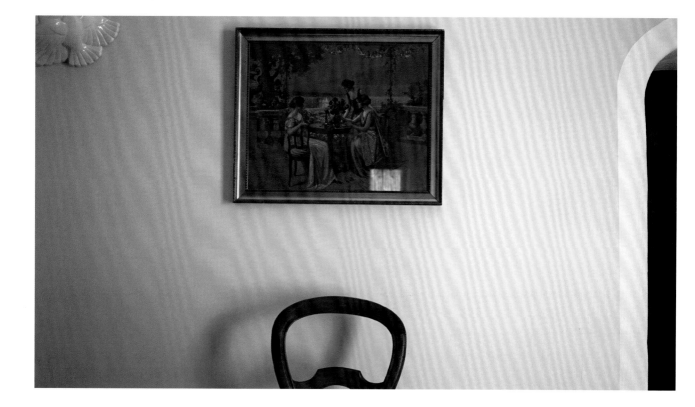

TOENAILS

She was skinny. Blonde. Long hair. Bright eyes. She was so kind. So open. I was eighteen.

I am sixty-eight and a half now, and she is sixty-seven. And we still kiss like kids. I am not afraid of my age. I am not embarrassed.

For years, she would lie on top of me to fall asleep. Now, we hold hands. Sex is not love. We waited three years before doing it.

Our first daughter was born handicapped. And when Paule discovered she couldn't have children again, we adopted two kids. We are an extremely tight-knit family. But they are adults now; they have their own lives.

In the winter, Paule and I go to the southeast of France. In the Ardèche region. Far from everything. We lock ourselves up to be just the two of us, alone, surrounded by the snow and the silence.

We want to die together. We want to get in our bed, embrace, look at each other for a very, very long time; smile.

"Forever will I love you."

Exhale.

*Xavier Grech, 68, retired aeronautical engineer*

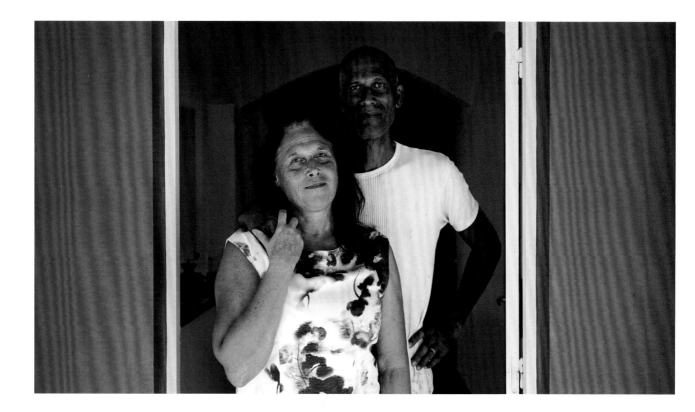

# RUBICON

*La Trinité, Martinique*

*Si ou pa dòmi an poulayé, ou pa sav si poul ka wonflé.* It's Creole. It means: "If you've never slept in the hen house, you will never know if the hens are snoring." And that's exactly what is happening in homes—you just can't guess what is going on.

I was living in hell. In a prison. My wife was always yelling at me. If I didn't buy garlic at the supermarket because there wasn't any left, she would rush back there to check whether I was lying or not. In the morning, we would drive together to the train station, but I would go sit at the front of the train and she would sit at the back.

I was so afraid to leave her. I was afraid of the unknown. I had married for better or for worse. And the worst had happened. So I resolved to die of sadness. Slowly. And I prepared my will.

But one day, I saw her. It was on rue Jean-Jacques Rousseau in Paris. She was wearing a blue dress with flowers. I couldn't help it: "Bonjour, Madame." A few days later, I was on the bus to meet Myriam for lunch.

How was I going to cross the rubicon? I had never cheated on my wife, but I had a dream. A dream in which my father told me: "Sylvain, climb this mountain. At the top, you'll see a little house. Go inside." That same night, Myriam dreamed of my father too. She had never seen him, but he was there—tall, thin, with his long hair, looking at her. He told her to open a gate. And when she did, there was a field of poppies, and I was there, standing in the middle of the flowers, waiting for her.

We have been married for ten years. But I always have this pain in me. If Myriam raises her voice the tiniest bit, I get scared. But then, she looks at me and says: "It's me, Sylvain. It's Myriam. I'm here for you."

*Sylvain Thalmensy, 62, retired policeman,*
*and Myriam Thalmensy, 59, nonprofit coordinator*

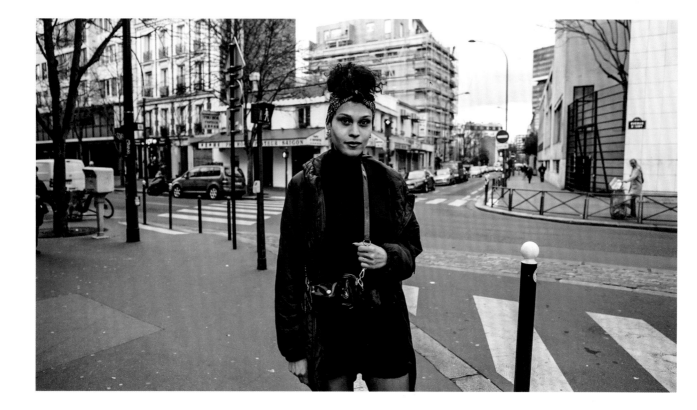

# WEATHER

*Paris, Paris*

I spent all the money I had left on two buckets of fried chicken for eight people, and I ate them all. I gathered all my anxiolytics, and I swallowed them all. I went to the window and jumped, from the seventh floor.

I woke up the next day at the hospital. I had landed on my neighbors' terrace. I weighed 375 pounds, and my fat cushioned the fall.

I survived. My friends asked: "Who do you want to be?"

I always knew who I was. I was a woman.

And that's when I started my transition.

Love wasn't for me. Really, who would love a monster? I had no idea who I was. I had friends and my art; that was enough for me. But I started losing weight, having curves, and I realized I was attractive. Men started looking at me. I began to experience all the problems women suffer from. Harassment. Flashing. I was very much on social media, and I posted a lot of pictures of myself on Instagram. And men would try to seduce me by sending me messages. I mostly told them to get lost, but I didn't with him. I didn't with Anthony.

We talked for six months before we met. He lived between France and Portugal. I fell in love with the feelings that all his messages stirred in me. When I came home from work, I wouldn't call my friends anymore; I would text him. And one day, he said it: "I am coming to Paris. I want to meet you." We did, at a train station. A neutral location. When he saw me, he sat next to me. I couldn't say a word. "Say something," he said. Nothing, I couldn't. So he kissed me. My first kiss. At twenty-five years old.

We walked for hours. Same thing the next day and the day after. I didn't even go to work anymore. After a week, I asked: "Want to go to my place?" We had never talked about my trans identity. I thought it was weird. So I told him. He was so uncomfortable; I asked him to leave.

No news from him.

Two weeks later, he's at my door with flowers: "I'm sorry. I'm an idiot. I want you to meet my

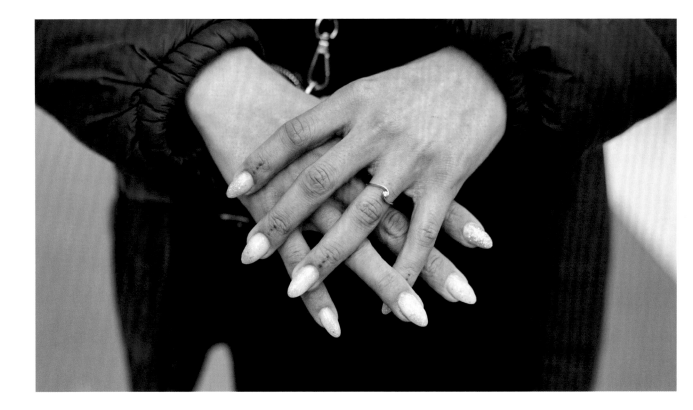

parents, my friends. I want you to know who I am." And that's how it started.

But he had broken my trust, so I had to know everything about him and have access to all his devices. And I dug, I dug, I dug. But there was nothing to dig for. What I found was extraordinary: messages to his parents where he said I made him happy no matter who I was or who I am today.

When I met him, he was letting himself die. I helped him open up to the world. Find a job. He made his own transition: to be happy. And he helped me trust myself. Once a month, he puts Post-its all over the apartment, and one after the other, we read them out loud: "Love yourself," "Breathe," "You are pretty."

I love when he makes me breaded chicken. When he sleeps at night, he smells like my childhood teddy. And when he gets out of the shower, he smells like good weather.

But then, the anxieties come back. I still have a lot of surgery to go through. And I'm afraid he won't love me when I finally change sex. I have heard so many stories of people leaving their partners.

But he gave me his heart, and I gave him mine. He asked me to marry him. I said yes. He got me a very simple ring: "You are always touching your hair, so I didn't want it to hurt you."

*Claude-Emmanuelle Gajan-Maull, 28,*
*store manager and artist*

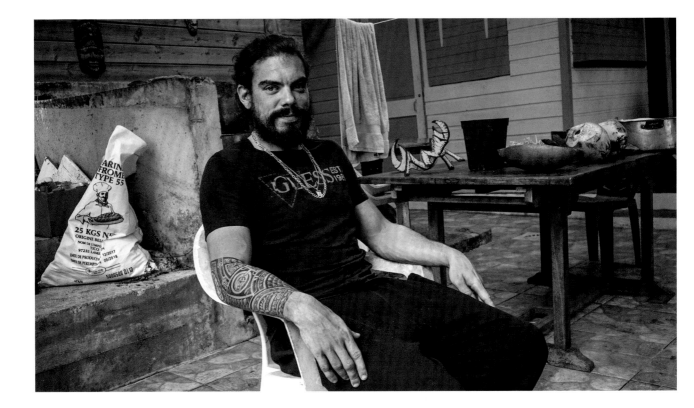

# BODY

*Le Diamant, Martinique*

When I was a young man, I had no self-confidence. I didn't like my body. I was scared of not being a good lover. Fear paralyzed me. If I liked a girl, I couldn't articulate a word. I was afraid of not having anything interesting to say. Or of looking too dumbstruck.

Truth is, I thought I could never attract love.

My friends and I would never talk about feelings. We weren't allowed to be fragile. And so I suffered. Too afraid to abandon this image of a strong man. Because if I did, it meant I was weak.

But then I met her. And she loved me back. She opened my heart. She helped me open up. To be myself.

I wanted to settle. But it scared her, and she left. It deeply wounded me. I couldn't eat. I couldn't sleep. I lost a piece of myself with her.

We were so young. If only I had met her today.

I have been with other women over the years.

I even got into a civil union. But that woman curbed my freedom.

I have been single for a year. I'm not a womanizer. I don't want to have lots of sexual experiences. What I want is connection. Affection. I miss being loved. I miss the emotion. I miss having a feminine presence.

I miss the tenderness.

It's hard out here. Love is not like in Disneyland.

Still, I have never been this happy. Even if I am on my own, I have never felt so free. I am finally the man I have always wanted to be. And I have never felt so honest with myself.

I am a tree trimmer. And last night, I went into the forest, I put up my hammock, and I fell asleep.

Alone.

*Jonathan Fenoy, 32, tree trimmer*

# SHIT

*Saint-Léger-sur-Dheune, Saône-et-Loire*

I met him when I was living in New York. He was working in the deli downstairs from my office. He asked me out for coffee. The first thing he said was that I was old, and the second thing was that he didn't like girls who smoked. But I was very attracted to this tall, brown-haired man. During our third date, he said he wanted to have children with me. I liked that he was sensitive, and I let my guard down.

The day we got married, he became a different person. I moved to France, and for a while, he stayed in the United States. My mother organized a surprise weekend to a spa for the two of us and my sister. And when I called to tell him about it, he said: "Did you ask for my permission?" Then, on my birthday, he called and told me that he had had sex with another woman the previous night. I was hurt and angry, and I had sex with a man myself. But I felt so guilty.

He moved to Paris to live with me. I wasn't really happy, but I thought: "Let's see how it goes." It started immediately: "Your apartment is shit. Your life is shit. You are fat." He even became violent. I thought it was my fault, that he was right, that I was chubby and not very pretty. But he had chosen me, this extraordinary man. One minute, he would praise me, and the next, he would insult me.

I got pregnant. And I thought, "Maybe if we build a family, it will get better." It didn't.

When my baby girl was two months old, he threw her into her crib. I had to protect her. I left.

So that's my love story. Suffering.

*Céline Levi-Chebat, 46, project coordinator*

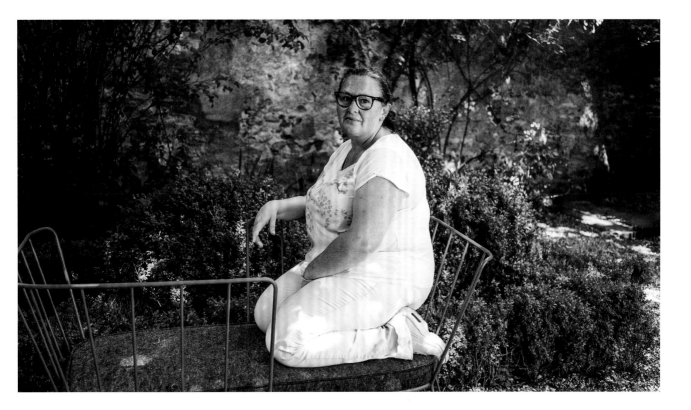

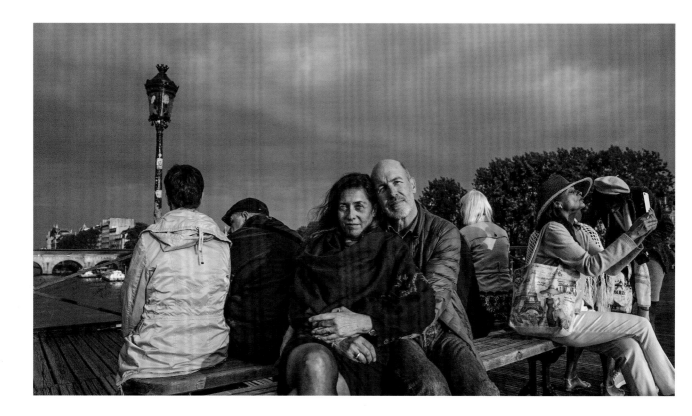

# COMFORT

*Paris, Paris*

I was brought up in a bourgeois family, and my mom was obsessed with money. It was the only thing that mattered. But I wasn't rich enough compared to my other friends, so when it was time to get married, I was despised by my girlfriend's parents. They made me feel like an outcast. I understood that I was always going to be scorned by my own people.

So I decided to marry a simple woman. Someone with whom my money wasn't going to be a problem. Someone with whom I could have the upper hand. And I met Marie. She was from the countryside. She was beautiful, gentle, and sensitive. Her family loved me. Her father sat me down next to him and poured me good wine. We got married.

I am pessimistic and negative. I am not altruistic. I have so little confidence in myself that I always have to be in control. I get very emotional, and I yell all the time. At her, at the kids. I can be so mean, and I don't even realize it.

But Marie always knows how to talk to me and to calm me down. She always pushes me to get to the bottom of the problem. She never leaves me alone. I think the problem is solved, but no, she will bring it up again. Sometimes it helps, but most of the time, she wants to have the last word. It's exhausting. I have wanted to divorce her so many times, but she has always found a way to hold me back. Because of that, I suffer a lot. Because of that, I love her.

For years, I didn't feel loved by Marie. When I would tell her I loved her, she wouldn't answer. There are days where I still have that feeling. But she was depressed and was suffering so much. And even though she didn't love me back, she gave me the tenderness I was looking for. Because I wasn't looking for her love, really; I was looking for a mother. For comfort. Mine never took care of me, never held me in her arms.

I love Marie like a child, naively. Last week, I put my hand on her shoulder, and she told me she liked it when I did that.

*Philippe Ventadour, 65, project manager*

I come from a farm. From a simple life. I wanted out. So I studied hard, and after a couple of years I moved to Paris. The night I arrived, I met Philippe. He was handsome. He was bourgeois. He was modest and discreet. He was the one.

Our wedding day was hell. Why? Because we had decided to get married on a whim. I was pregnant. I lost the baby fifteen days before the ceremony. The atmosphere was bleak. Dark. My parents weren't there because we had rushed to get wed. I felt alone. I wasn't good enough for Philippe's friends.

Philippe was yelling all the time. He was vulgar. I was afraid of him. With the kids, it was the same. I was always doing things wrong; it was never his way.

But I had seen my father yell at my mom, and I knew that at the end of the day, he was a good man. They never separated, and I liked that. I had made myself the promise that I would never leave my husband if I were to get married one day. Now that I was, I was ready to get to work.

I knew Philippe was a good man. Each fight, each reconciliation was a step forward. Was it all worth it? I don't know. It sounds Machiavellian, but it was my choice. A man who yells is a child who screams for help, who needs assistance. And I helped him grow; he never grew up really.

I suffer from depression. Philippe never judged me for it, but he never really understood what I had, and it was very painful for me to see him trivialize my disease. But when I was going through times of crisis, he was very good to me and attentive. He managed everything, including the children. After ten years, doctors finally diagnosed me with bipolar disorder, and I have been getting treatment ever since. It's opened my eyes to how much I love him.

What does he give me? Love, I can feel it. Support. Admiration. Everything a woman wants, I have it. Except we don't share much. We don't do anything together. He likes to go biking, read the newspapers, watch rugby. I like to go to a museum, to the movies. We don't like the same music; we don't watch the same shows. We are together when we sit down for dinner, when we cook—that's when we talk.

We are still learning to love each other. I am proud of where I brought him. I push him constantly. I know what is good for him. I will never leave him in peace.

*Marie Ventadour, 60, midwife*

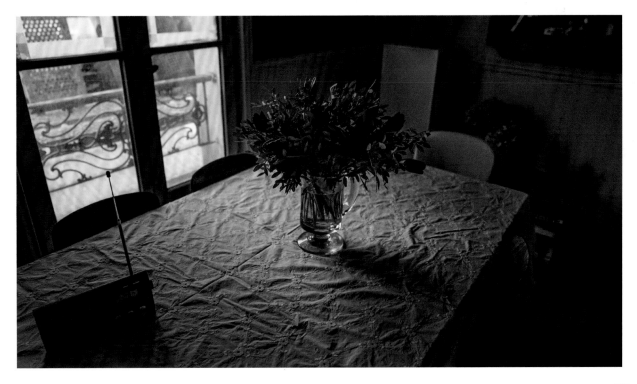

# FLESH

*Montfaucon, Gard*

We met online fourteen years ago. He had just been dumped and didn't want to be with anyone, but his best friend had secretly created his profile on a website. We met up at a party. I went back home to his house, and I never left. It was a Saturday. That Monday, his mother and sister came over for lunch!

I had been married before, for fifteen years. And we had had two children together.

I always knew I was gay. But at the time, it was hard to come out, and I did love her. She eventually realized I liked men, and we divorced.

Hervé and I were the first gay couple to get married in the Gard region.

Hervé's best friend, a lesbian, asked him if he could help her girlfriend have a baby. He accepted on the condition that he would be the father and involved in raising the child. She was inseminated and got pregnant right away. Axelle was born.

But she and her girlfriend went crazy and didn't want to share the custody. They accused us of being pedophiles. It was hell.

This was Hervé's child, his flesh and blood.

We didn't see her for a whole year.

We went to court and won shared custody. She is nine years old today.

Love is getting older together. It is the family we built together.

This year for Father's Day, for the first time, Axelle's teacher had her make a present for each of us.

*Patrick Millot-Gustave, 54, secretary,*
*and Hervé Millot-Gustave, 54, accountant*

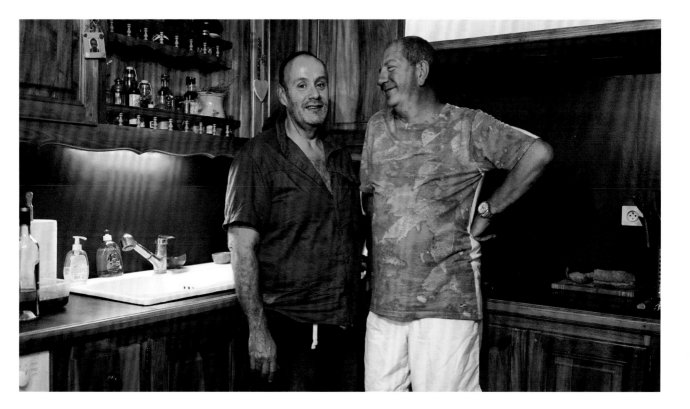

# TRANSFER

*Ernestviller, Moselle*

My father told me: "You will never leave this house until you get married." I met Alain when I was eighteen years old. We would hook up every year at summer camp. Eventually, we decided to get married. I was young; I needed to break free of my father.

We moved here, to Ernestviller, in this big house. I didn't want to. It was imposed on me. It was lost in the middle of nowhere. It was too big. I didn't feel good. For one whole year, I didn't even go upstairs.

When I gave birth to my first child, my father came to the hospital. He sat down and said: "Now that you have a kid, you can get divorced."

Alain died brutally at thirty-eight years old. He had a heart attack. We were a good team. It was more friendship than love. But in a second it was all gone. Everything fell apart. Everything. I was all alone with my two kids.

I was working full time. I wish I had been there more for my kids. But I had to work, for them. And I didn't want to owe anything to anyone. Certainly not to my in-laws, who resented me for being alive. My mother-in-law, especially.

My pride, I say it loud and clear, is to have succeeded with my children. The rest, I don't give a damn. I gave them all the love my parents did not give me.

We are very close. Before any of them had serious girlfriends, I said, "Before it becomes impossible, let's go on vacation, just the three of us." We went to Greece. One night, they sat me down. "Mom. We have something to tell you. We don't want you to take care of us anymore." They were twenty-two and nineteen. I was fifty. I burst into tears. What was I going to do with my life? It was over, done. They were all I had left.

So I learned to live again. Differently. To live alone. To live without them. Without harassing them. Without their presence. To live for myself. It was a tough time.

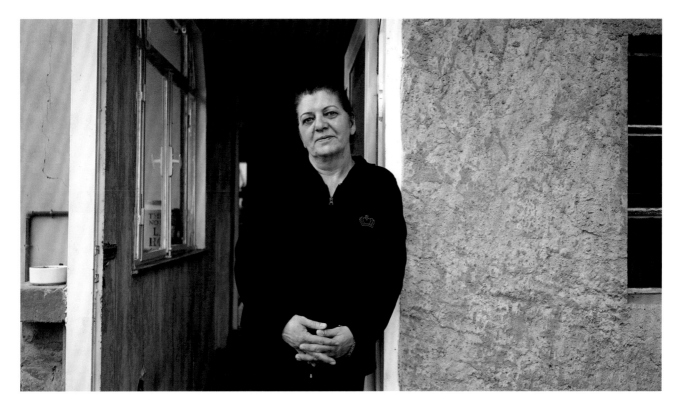

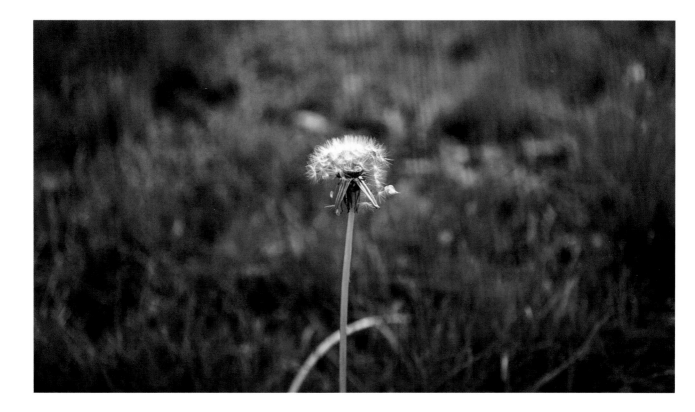

TRANSFER

One of my sons' friends said something great: "Your mom has to move out of her town because there are no more memories to create there." And that was exactly it. This house used to be full every weekend. A birthday, a party. But he was right.

I just asked for my transfer. It's a good thing. I am finally going to get to know myself.

*Anne Siebert, 55, executive assistant*

# FRIEND

*Sainte-Rose, Guadeloupe*

We met in the subway. In Paris. At the Place d'Italie stop. I had just turned twenty. I had never noticed him before. I was busy walking to work. But he had—noticed me. For weeks. He finally walked up to me: "Are you from Guadeloupe?"

I was.

We've spent every day together since. And it's been forty-three years.

When we met, I would write letters to my parents every week to tell them how I was doing. We didn't have cell phones at the time, nor internet. And one day, Dony asked me for their address. He wanted to write them a letter too. To ask my father's permission to marry me.

Dony hasn't changed since the day we met. Aggressiveness is not our thing; warmth is. Dony is very calm. He never gets angry or loud. And when we disagree, we always sit and talk about it.

He is messy, and I am not. I love to talk, and he never tells me to keep quiet.

We don't have to reassure ourselves or be kissy all the time. We never tell each other that we love each other. I know I have his back, and he has mine.

Today, love is ephemeral. People divorce so quickly, and they don't try to solve their problems. It's always the other person's fault. They never question themselves.

I don't have any friends.

I did have some when I was a kid.

I have acquaintances and am happy to see them, but other than that, it's only him.

He's my only friend.

*Suzy Diakok, 66, retired secretary,*
*and Dony Diakok, 69, retired mail carrier*

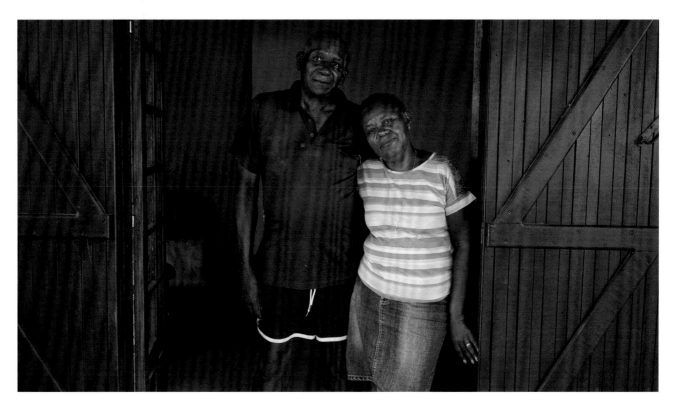

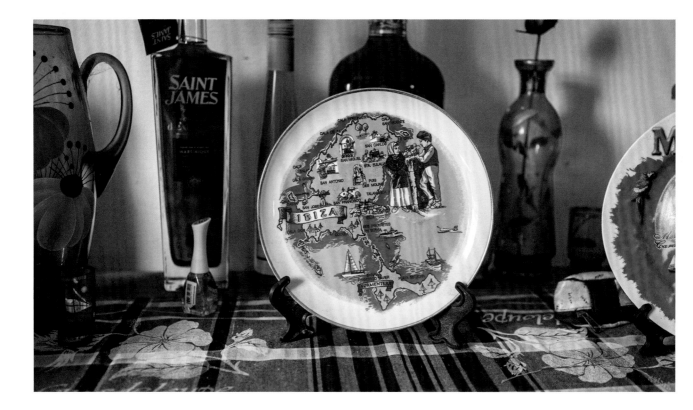

FRIEND

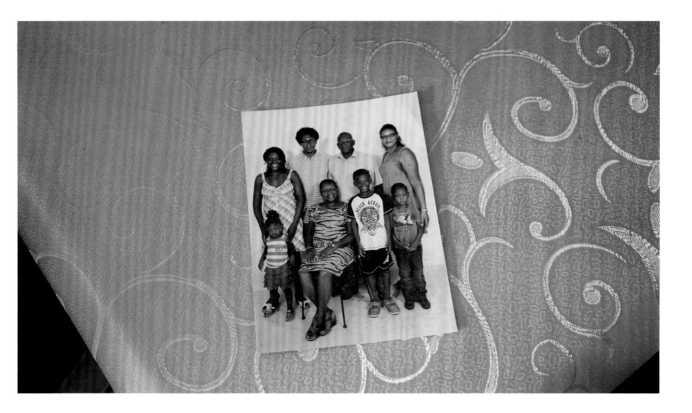

# Breakfast

*Champeix, Puy-de-Dôme*

I met him when I was eighteen years old. My parents had introduced us. We got married. But then he got very sick. A serious illness: debilitating obsessive-compulsive disorder. He would obsess about whether his collar was turned the right way or whether our daughter's head was round enough. It was too much to bear: the psychiatric hospital, his emotional blackmail, his threats of suicide. I couldn't recognize the man I had fallen in love with. So I left. And I became the bitch who abandoned her husband.

But I became so lonely. And one day, I went grocery shopping and picked up one of those free crappy magazines and came across the personal ads. And there was Daniel's. It was so simple, I savored it. "An honest man looking for love." I woke up in the middle of the night thinking about the ad.

At 6:00 a.m., I was writing him a letter.

We have been together for seventeen years.

Is there love? I don't know. There always has been affection and tenderness between us. A routine. Support.

But there is no passion. And I can't live without it.

I met another man. At the gym. And I love him. He is married too.

Is there really one way of life? I don't think so. We have to stop pretending. Being hypocrites. We must be free.

I am free, even if it's very heavy to bear.

I don't want to leave Daniel. We are partners. We built our house, our social network. I don't want to break that. I told him about my lover. He accepted it. I also told my kids. They accepted it. Sometimes, we are having breakfast, and his name slips out, but we pretend nothing happened.

*Arlette Girard-Nugier, 55,*
*culture and events coordinator*

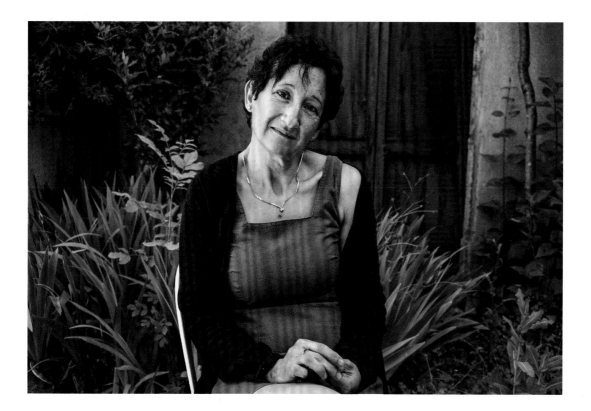

# CANDLES

*Megève, Haute-Savoie*

I first fell in love when I was nineteen. But after two years, she dumped me. I think I was too romantic for her. I did everything she wanted, and it bored her. Women are complicated: you do everything to make them happy, and they are uninterested; you don't care, and they love you.

I met my second love. I would take her out for dinner in very chic, very romantic restaurants, with nice views and candles everywhere. I really liked doing that. I was trying not to fall in love this time, but after three months, I did. When I'm in a relationship, I'm very passionate. There is no middle ground. It's all or nothing.

But without warning, she dumped me. It was horrible. I took all my stuff and left—hoping she would miss me and tell me to come back. It was a total failure.

I am single. It's been a year. And my trust in women has faded. I loved my girlfriends so much, but I felt betrayed, so I'm wondering: "Why should I give myself to them if they are going to hurt me?" I'm on a dating app, but I'd rather meet a girl organically, not by swiping right. It just feels good to know I have matches.

The truth is, I am scared of getting hurt. Because what I really think is that life is meant to be shared with that one person. I really would love to start a family.

But I'm alone, and I'm miserable.

*Thibault Grillet, 26, courier and chauffeur*

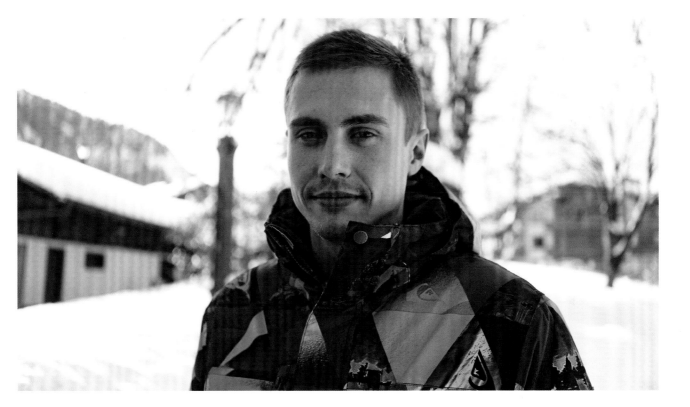

# FAMILY

*Le François, Martinique*

Just like my mother did with my dad, my ex-wife left me without warning. I got so angry at women. But also, so depressed.

I saw an ad on TV about a dating app, Tinder. I hated it. It wasn't for my generation. But I signed up.

I was living in Martinique, and I went to France to visit my mother. I got stuck in traffic. Laetitia's village was right next to the highway. Since the app is location based, she appeared on my feed. And we matched. I knew I had to fly back home, but I told her I was feeling lonely. She asked me why, and we started talking.

After weeks and weeks of writing to each other, I knew it. "I love you," I said. We had never met yet. And I am not the type of person who opens up. I am usually reserved. My parents never told me they loved me.

I asked her: "Can you wait for me?" She said yes. I flew back to France. And there she was at the airport. When I saw her, I dropped my suitcases, took her in my arms, and kissed her. She moved to Martinique with her children. It's been three years.

One month ago, my father died. I had always thought my family were my parents, but with him gone, that wasn't the case anymore. I sat down last week for dinner and told Laetitia and the kids: "You are my family now."

*Nicolas Poiret, 42, physical education teacher,*
*and Laetitia Enos, 33, nutritionist*

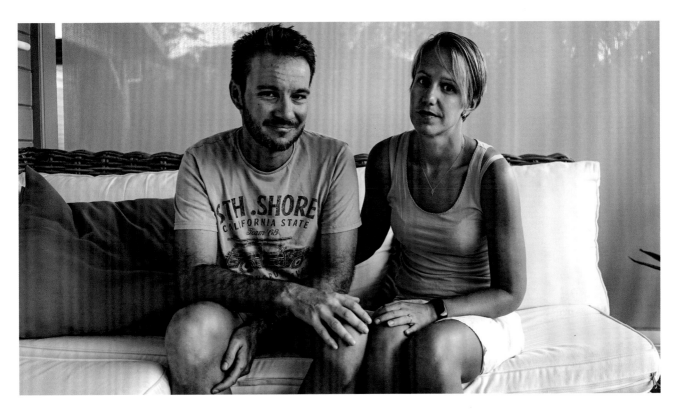

# PAINTING

*Marseille, Bouches-du-Rhône*

I have always kept my feelings on a leash. I have high moral values, but I am incapable of feeling that love you read about in books. That passion. I just don't know how to feel it.

But it doesn't stop me from loving Leïla.

We met ten years ago in university. I was a virgin. I wasn't looking to fall in love with a girl before sleeping with her. No. I was really sexually frustrated. But I also didn't want to break a girl's trust in me just for sex. Because I had always been the confidant.

One night, we all gathered to watch a horror movie, *The Hills Have Eyes*. She was drunk, and one of our friends was trying to kiss her. She didn't want to. So I helped her out. Then, everyone started dancing. And there she was—so beautiful in her white pants. I didn't dance. I didn't know how to. I still don't. Then, she sat next to me. Closer. She desired me. And I desired her. A mutual feeling, unprecedented for me. We made love that night. My first time.

But then, I was cold with her. Distant. She left me. It didn't really matter. I wasn't in love.

A few years later, I was on a train to meet up with my father, and there she was. She came to my house, in Avignon. We made love and went to the theater. For years after that, we would meet up at the same time of the year. And every summer meant sex with Leïla. Theater. And good wine. Until that July. She had just dumped her Italian lover and came over to my house. This time, she stayed. She didn't have to—but she did. After nine years, we were finally together. It's been a year now.

I am in love with her. I am in love with her bad moods. I love that she is complicated. She is the first person I have been in love with. I was just too centered on myself before that. But I am still the same man. I'm pragmatic. I'm rational. No lyrical musings. No romance.

Love for me is like a painting you are going to put up on your wall for twenty years. And each time you're going to look at it, you are going to see a new detail.

And that is exactly how I see Leïla.

*Lucas-Victor Ibsen, 28, tattoo artist,*
*and Leïla Quintin, 29, teacher*

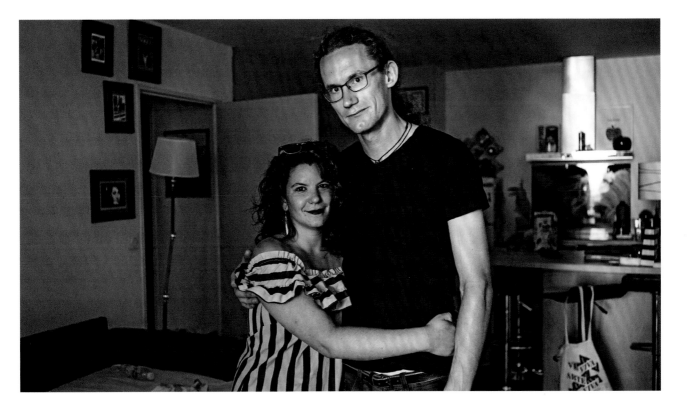

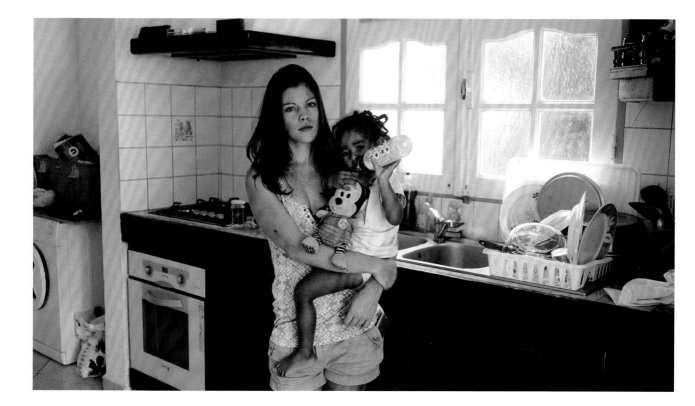

# MIA

*Sainte-Rose, Guadeloupe*

We were both working in the same hotel. I was twenty-two. He was thirty-six. I wanted to have fun, drink, and party. So did he. Six months later, I was pregnant. It was an accident. I wanted to get an abortion. He was getting more and more violent verbally. More and more drunk. More and more absent.

But then, I started loving what was growing inside of me. I kept her. But I didn't want to leave him. I couldn't imagine raising this baby alone. Or giving birth alone. It was too hard for me.

One day, I discovered he had been on a swingers app for months. He denied everything. Why did he hide it from me? Maybe I would have gone with him. It was constant lies. He was so mean.

He never included me in his life. And after three years, I just had to leave him.

It took me so many bad guys to get this confident. I think I was always looking for a man with the strong character I didn't have. I had to fight them. And that taught me to be tough and to say no. I have worked all my life to feel free and be free. And now I am. At last.

Today, it's just me and Mia. She is two years old. And sometimes, when I look at her, I cry with joy.

*Blandine Mazé, 26, hotel marketing manager, and Mia Mazé, 23 months old*

# WHERE

*Saint-Suliac, Ille-et-Vilaine*

I've been with women from all around the world. My first partner was Italian. The second, British. The third, Chinese. Then Swiss. After that, French. This last one would wait for me to fall asleep to log on to dating sites. I broke up with her. I sold my house and bought a new one.

But I was lonely, so I got back together with her. She started going on dating sites again, so I threw her out, again, and kept our dog.

Now, I sort of have a girlfriend. She works in a restaurant in Saint-Malo. She is young, twenty-seven years old. I'm also interested in my neighbor. She is twenty-three years old. She is six feet tall and weighs 165 pounds. She is charming. She's a veterinarian. Nothing has happened yet, but I am going to let her seduce me. Her boyfriend lives in Angers.

So what is love? Nothing for the moment. Love is no longer a goal when you reach sixty-eight. My love is my dog.

The one true love is the one you have for your children. I cry, because I lost my son.

Two, three times a month, I pick up flowers in my garden, in the street, anywhere, and I throw them in the ocean. I don't talk to him. I stand there crying.

He came to visit me in Aix-en-Provence, and he died on his motorcycle coming back from a nightclub. He had met a girl and had only one helmet that he gave to her. She survived.

He was thirty when it happened. At home, there are pictures of him everywhere. He was my friend. He was very cool.

He was much more handsome than I am, so with girls, I couldn't compete.

We rode our motorcycles all over the world together.

The first time I went overseas after the accident, I rode my bike in Ireland. And every night, I would look for him. I would ask myself: "Where is he? Where is he?"

*Christian Juin, 68, retired photographer*

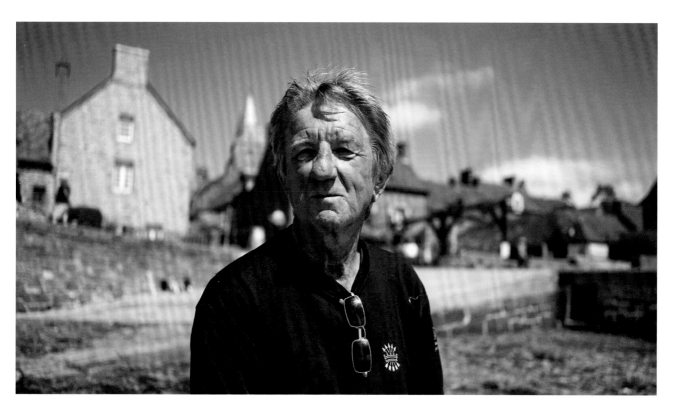

# WAR

*Épinal, Vosges*

I was in the military for fifteen years. I was in Central America and the Middle East. I became addicted to Pervitin, which I took to avoid falling asleep. I was just so afraid of dying. I would shoot at any car that would get too close to us.

I came home from Afghanistan in 2009. I became anorexic. I had been married for fifteen years. She left. She just couldn't handle it.

She is the last person I have been in love with. I have been single since then. It has been five years.

My heart is an abyss, and I want to fill it. I would love to have just a little attention; I am not too demanding.

Seeing happy people pisses me off, because I am not. I am so angry. I have everything: a good body, a car, a house, a full bank account. But I don't have the essential thing: love. And on the few dates I've had, I felt like a walking wallet. Women are vile, treacherous, and incapable of expressing a simple thing: they go from point A to point B while taking a detour by point Z, like a plane that circles around its target.

I never understand what they want. For me, it's black or white; there is no gray. Gray is fog; you can't see through it. Maybe I am too direct, too cold, too rigid. I don't know what seduction is. Maybe I am an anomaly. For me, seduction is energy spent for an uncertain result. Love is simple, honest, and sane; chatter is useless. You get to know someone by living with them. You get the gut feeling, or not.

I live in a small town, so it's hard to meet people. I have five friends. I am going to wait for a woman to come to me. Because if it fails, I can hold her responsible.

Every day, I feel sad. Loneliness is worse than the atomic bomb.

I try to keep busy: reading, writing, video games, sports. I go shoot my machine guns once in a while. I am not depressed anymore. I don't take pills, because I don't want to be addicted to anything ever again.

Last time I cried was last Christmas, because I was alone. I am going to be alone this year too.

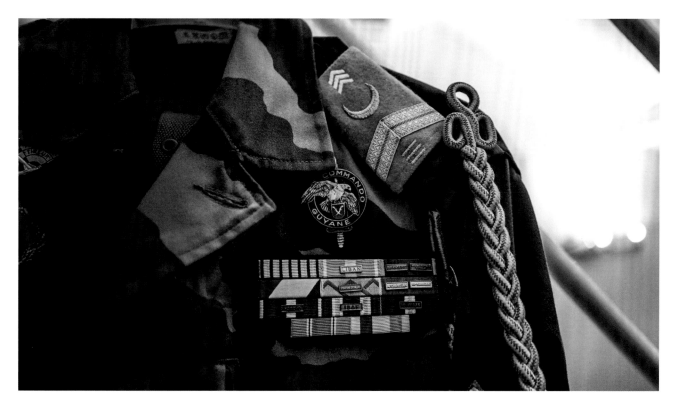

Sometimes, I think I am paying for all the atrocities that I committed all over the world. I have killed. I have tortured. I have hardened myself so much to protect my heart, and it's going to be very hard for the person I meet to strip away that armor.

I miss war. The adrenaline. I could go back and work freelance. I have enough days of paid vacation to go fight in any conflict zone for two months and two weeks.

*Jean Lauriot*, 40, health personnel manager*

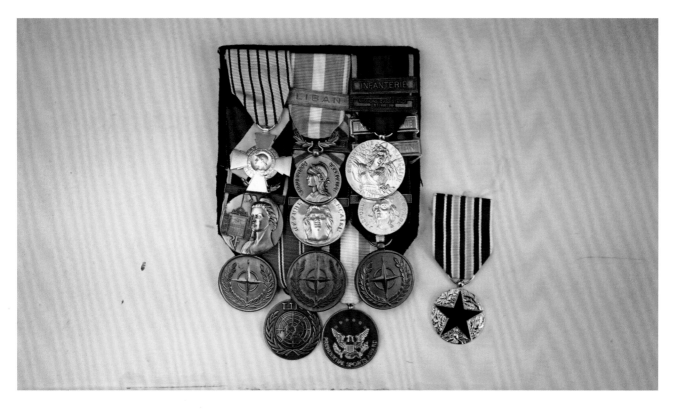

# Naked

*Les Houches, Haute-Savoie*

I'm a mailwoman. I had been delivering mail to Christian's house for years. He had always been nice to me, but I never liked him in that way. We would even go on hikes together. But then, over the years, it changed. He was just so kind to me. This summer, I needed help with my house, and it happened: a quick little kiss on the lips. I hadn't been kissed by a man in years.

The man I had been married to for ten years didn't love me. He was cold from day one. I thought I loved him because he was a serious man. No bars, no girls. A workaholic. But he would never show any sign of affection, and he didn't want to kiss me.

I am now fifty-five. It took me twenty years to meet Christian. He takes care of me, he cooks, he is gentle. I want to see him every day, stay in bed with him. I have never been this comfortable sexually before. We walk around naked. You can't do that with just anyone.

But there is a problem. I get jealous. He is always talking about his exes and saying how great they are, or talking about this girl and saying how nice she is. It gives me huge stomach pains.

I don't know if I've ever told him I loved him. I am still waiting to tell him.

But until today, I didn't know what it was to be loved.

*Marie Devey, 55, mail carrier*

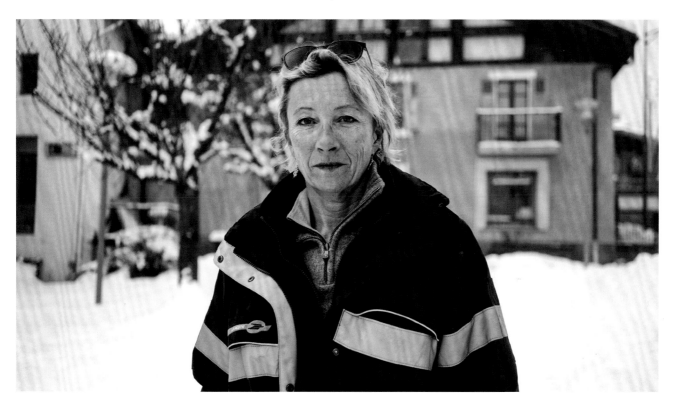

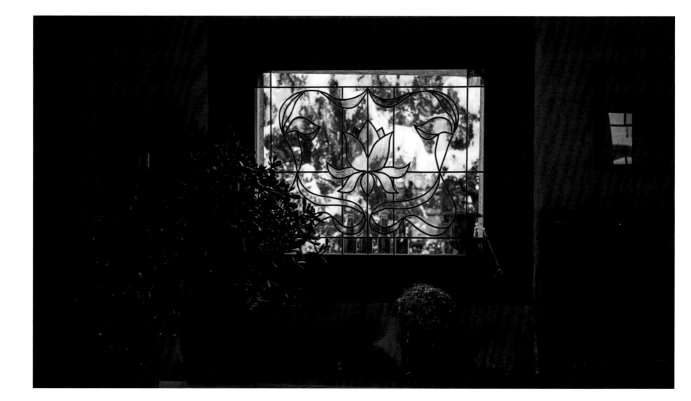

NAKED

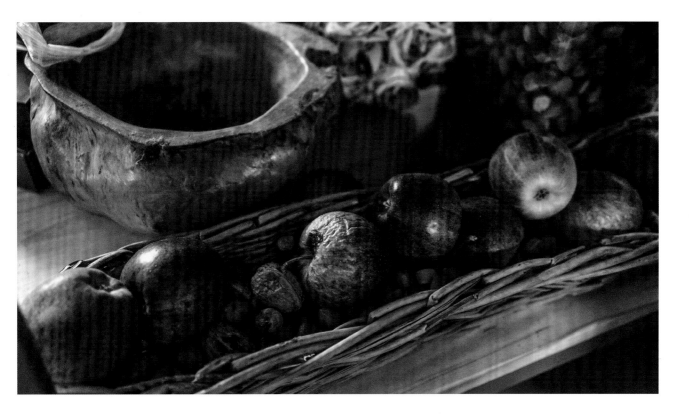

# FORGIVENESS

*Paris, Paris*

My mom gave me condoms when I turned sixteen. All my friends were having sex. I wasn't. I was so stressed out about it. But the fear of failure was stronger than the hormones. So I lied—to everyone; I was a very good liar. I lost my virginity when I was twenty-two, not seventeen. And I never told the girl I lost my virginity to that she was my first.

I had very little confidence. I still do. I fell in love with the strong girls, the ones with a lot of character. I thought love was something that was intense, that grabbed you by the throat. But I confused dysfunction with strength. The two women I fell in love with didn't treat me well. They were mean. Screaming. Humiliating me. I always thought I was doing things wrong, and I would ask them for forgiveness.

But these women were giving me attention. They made me feel as if I existed. So I loved them. And I stayed, even if I had to suffer.

Until I met Coline. She was having a drink with a friend of mine. She was wearing glasses, and I love girls with glasses. Her curls were going in all directions. At a party, the next day, she kissed me. I moved out of my girlfriend's house, and Coline moved back to Paris. We were both living at our parents' for a while, so we would meet up in the street and make out like teenagers.

It wasn't love at first sight with Coline. My love for her built slowly. She is radiant and funny. She's always kissing and hugging me. We talk, a lot. There is no jealousy. There is a real flow to our love. And I am finally myself.

I realized, thanks to Coline, that love is calm.

*Gabriel Gauffre, 32, photographer*

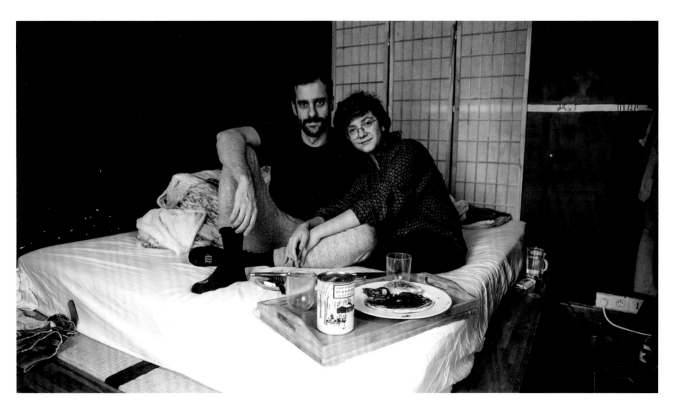

The first time we had a coffee together, we spoke for hours—as if we had always known each other. I felt very strange after that: my hands were shaking, and I couldn't get him off my mind. That same night, I kissed him. He had a girlfriend and I was seeing someone too, but for some reason, being together felt very normal, natural.

I went back to London; he went back to Paris. We spoke a lot on Facebook Messenger. I was moving back to France, and I would send him pictures of my rock collections, of my feet. Just as I would with a friend, but with feelings. We met again for a photography workshop in Budapest. When we saw each other, we kissed on the cheeks, and that was it. We had never talked again about our kiss. We shared the same apartment. He was in the living room; I was in the bedroom. I was hoping he would join me in bed. He never did. But one night—after three days—we were telling each other scary stories through the door. And I thought, "That's it. I am going over there. One, two, three." I stood up and went to his bed. But we were lying down back to back. We were just like kids. We slowly turned around. He put his foot on mine. We held hands. Making that extra step meant the start of something important. I was scared. He was too.

We kissed.

The first three months, I wanted to leave him. I was afraid of my feelings for him. I didn't want to fall in love. I didn't want to be hurt. My ex had cheated on me, and it broke me. I would cry when I woke up in the morning, when I fell asleep. I had nightmares about him. My recovery was long and painful.

With Gabriel, I wrote drafts and drafts of texts where I told him it was over. I canceled dinner with him, because if I saw him, I would leave him. I was sabotaging our relationship. He had left a girl for me. "Was he going to do the same with me?"

But I stayed, and he proved me wrong. He takes care of me, and I take care of him. We both are vulnerable and not very self-confident, and I like that about us. I show him what he can't see in himself: that he's a great man. I know that if we have a problem, we will fix it—together.

Today, I am a bit lost in my career. In my life. I have no idea where I am heading. But I do know who I am going with. With Gabriel. I think we are all a bit lonely, and we give each other purpose. He is opening a new world to me: his world. And I love it. I love him. We are moving to China. It's going to be extraordinary.

*Coline Plançon, 28, education manager*

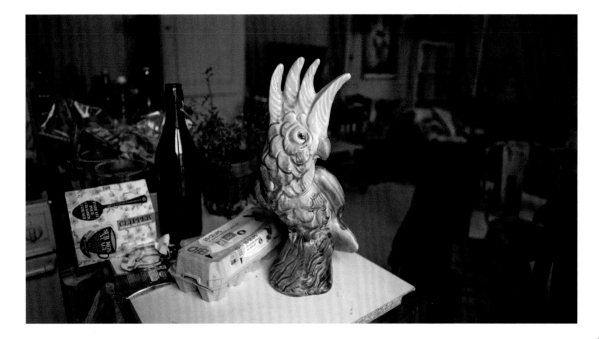

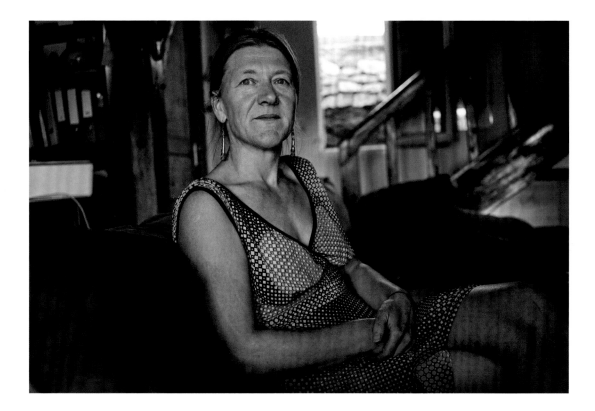

# KILL

*Montluçon, Allier*

I had failed my two previous relationships. I was alone. I was aimless. So I said yes to the first asshole I pitied. He wasn't feeling good, and I decided to save him. We met in October, and in November, he moved in. I learned the love of my life was getting married, which made me jealous enough to marry the asshole. If he could do it, I could do it.

But after six months, I realized I didn't love him. Then the harassment started. He never left me alone. Ever. He was such a perverse man, a manipulator, always making me feel like crap. He brought out the worst in me: the capacity to kill. We got in a huge fight, and I started strangling him. Very tightly. I was so wound up. And then, it suddenly hit me: "What am I doing?"

I got lucky. We broke up. And I fell in love again. With Benoît. I adore making love with him. I adore talking with him. He is so knowledgeable. I swear like a sailor. He never says a bad word.

Everything was rolling until Benoît—that bastard—decided to fuck his colleague in her truck. He felt so guilty, he had to tell me. Why did he do that? "Take your stuff, get out!" And when I said that, he fell in love again, just like the first day. So we got back together.

He just moved for a job. It's a good thing that he's gone. Because we miss each other again.

*Nathalie Henry, 48, neuropsychologist*

# FRUIT

*Le Vauclin, Martinique*

I have had feelings for a woman. But love? I don't really know what it is. I am not sure.

What I want is to give love. To give love to a lot of women. Warmth, sex, help. You can love several people at the same time. I think loving just one woman is possession. If you lose that one person, what are you left with? I want love to be simple.

I am free. I am free like a bird. I am free like a butterfly. I live alone. I built my house. I grew a garden. I planted all the fruit.

Do you want me to give you some love?

*José Pierre-Jérôme, 43, fisherman*

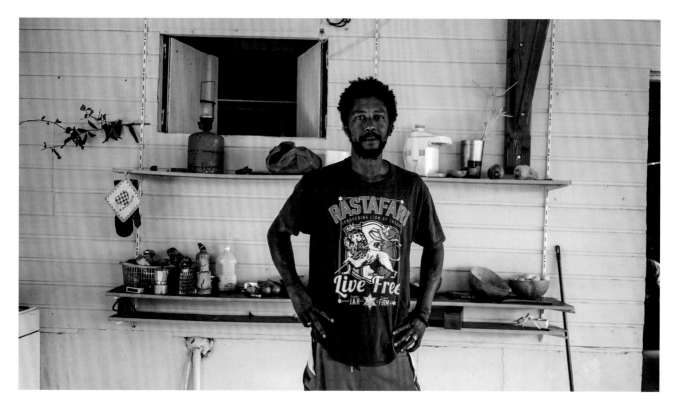

# CARE BEAR

*Saint-Denis-Catus, Lot*

We met at a ski station in 2009. We were both working at a hotel. He was a cook; I was cleaning rooms and working as a waitress. We would party a lot. One night, we hadn't even had anything to drink. It was impulsive. I went to his room. He was all alone. I pushed him against the wardrobe, kissed him passionately, and left. And that was it. I was with someone, and he had a crush on another girl.

Years later, we ended up back at the same hotel. We were both single. I had always idealized him. And I was thinking: "He would never like a girl like me. I wear baggy pants and listen to electronic music." But at the end of each party, we would always end up dancing together, slowly, holding each other tightly. Without kissing, without talking. Just hugging. And on Valentine's Day, he and a friend got the girls roses, very prince-like, and then we went to a nightclub. We kissed. It happened naturally.

He is the last romantic man of my generation. He gets me flowers. He opens the door. He pulls the chair out for me. He puts on "Unforgettable" by Nat King Cole to dance to. He has a pure heart, a pure soul. He's never told me to shut up or to fuck off.

I didn't want kids because I always thought, "I don't want to impose anything on a little pea who didn't ask for anything."

But that was before I met Vincent. I'm pregnant. He just bought me peanut butter and ginger biscuits.

I thought Prince Charming didn't exist. He does.

I lost my twin sister ten years ago in a car accident. So I knew what it was to be the other half of someone. Now, with him, I feel complete.

My sister had a pink Care Bear when she was born. Today, I can't sleep without it. Vincent bought me a second bear, a colorful patchwork bear, and told me: "This way your Care Bear will never be alone again."

*Amélie Le Bouleis, 31, and Vincent Labrousse, 31, owners of the restaurant Ô Grands Gourmands*

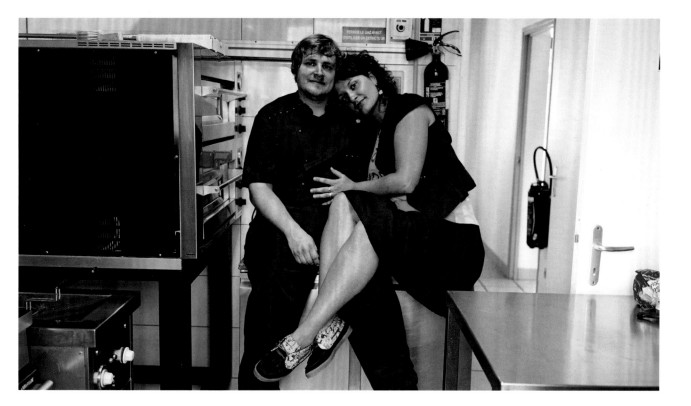

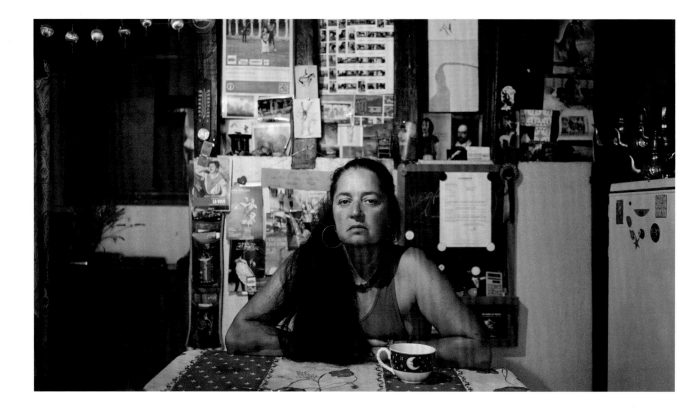

# HORSE

*Montbron, Charente*

He had the reputation of being a great charmer. All the girls wanted him. He went out with blonde duchesses or dancers with long legs. I, on the other hand, was the tiny girl with no money.

He made accessories for a circus company, and I was an equestrian performer. I would go barefoot on the horse's back, stand on it, or ride sidesaddle.

I fell in love with him, and he fell in love with me. I think I am the first girl he introduced to his parents.

I thought he represented security. He turned out to be the opposite. He did everything to make me feel bad about myself and dependent on him. He cheated on me. He took me away from my friends. He constantly belittled me.

I directed comedians and acrobats, but he would go behind my back to tell them my artistic direction was all wrong. All in a very cordial but very perverse way.

I started telling people what was going on, and no one helped me. "But you have such a strong character," they would tell me. And I kept trying to make it work. Because I was still in love. That's the trap.

Our son understood everything that was going on. He was the one who would bring me a glass of water after my husband would choke me.

We stayed together for seventeen years—until one day, he tried to strangle me and throw me out the window. I left him. He never apologized.

I do not believe that I am damaged by love, despite everything that I have lived through. I am strong and sensitive. I don't think I'm fragile. I would love to raise a second child. I have been given the green light to adopt one.

Today, I am living a new story. A beautiful story. I mean, I hope. I am with one of my old lovers. He had never left my mind. And when I saw him again, all the sensations were there, intact. He is a magnificent rider, flamboyant. Both of us love horses. It is in our blood.

I told him: "When you are ready, I will come pick you up in my car, I will take your hand, and we will go to city hall."

*Eva Schakmundès, 53, equestrian performer and carpenter*

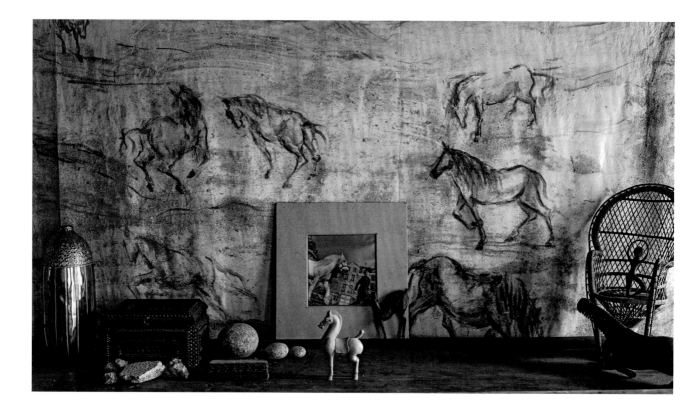

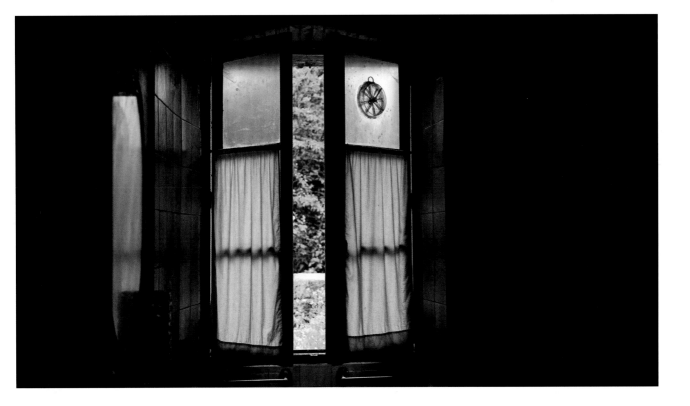

# ROLLER COASTER

*Montbron, Charente*

My parents were not at all a model of love. If I were to follow their example, I would be heading for disaster.

I am seventeen. I think at our age, we are discovering what love is: the first kiss, the first time having sex, the first hangovers together. You are sad, then you are happy, then angry. It's an emotional roller coaster.

My longest relationship lasted six months.

I believe in love. I want children. I want one with my partner, and I want to adopt one. I want to be able to talk to her in twenty-five years and remember all the great things we shared together.

My dream is to drive Route 66 in the United States with my best friend. And we've decided that if we get girlfriends, they would come with us.

I am the fun guy. I try not to be too invasive. You can ask me to talk to anyone—it doesn't scare me—but to talk about love? I totally lose my nerve. I am super shy. When I like a girl, it takes me such a long time to ask her out. I am all shaky, and I don't know what to do with myself.

There is this girl that I am in love with. Her name is Rose. She is one grade below me. I was so nervous that I sent her a text to ask her out. I know it's corny—I hate it! After you send a text, you are like: "Should I have sent it? Did I do the right thing?" I regret not asking her out directly. She said she wasn't looking for a boyfriend at the moment.

I get turned down all the time. I give up.

*Noé Laisné, 17, high school student and*
*Eva Schakmundès's son*

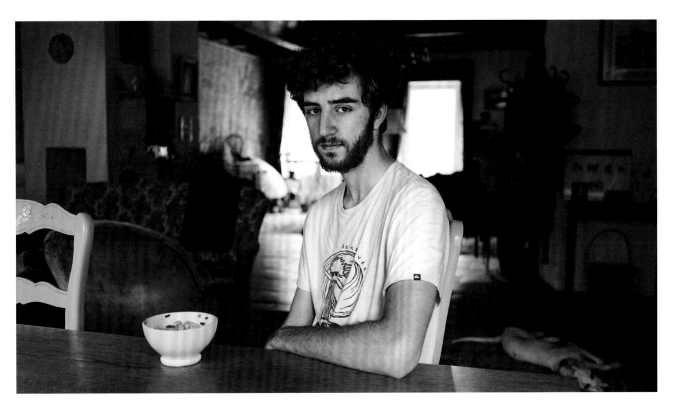

# RIB EYE

*Bedous, Pyrénées-Atlantiques*

I was a seasonal worker so I dated lots of women. But one night, I was at a dinner party, and Edith and I sat across from each other. It was love at first sight. Back at the camp, I woke my friend up and said: "I was against marriage, but I've changed my mind!" She was eighteen. I was twenty-five.

We only saw each other again a year later. I was working as a cook in her uncle's restaurant. We would talk in the kitchen, and I would bring her home on my bicycle. We were like magnets.

But I had planned to do a transatlantic sailing race with a friend, so I left.

A few weeks in, there were violent storms. We had no more food. We were in the middle of the ocean, but we might as well have been on the moon—fifteen days away from the shore. I thought I would never make it back.

On the boat, I imagined myself eating a rib-eye steak in the mountains in front of a fire. I also had this recurring dream where I was about to take a train. Edith was there. The train wasn't stopping so I had to throw my bags into the wagon without saying good-bye to her. But then I would think: "What are you doing?" And I would get off the train and stay with Edith.

That's when I realized I was on the wrong path. When we made it to shore, I immediately went to her. Edith and I met again at a train station at Christmas. We have been together for fourteen years. We've built two houses and have had three children.

Now, we are buying an old train station in our village to turn it into a hotel and a restaurant, where I will cook rib-eye steaks on a firepit in the middle of the mountains.

Everything is linked.

*Fabrice Moutengou-Dubuc, 39, cook,*
*and Edith Moutengou-Dubuc, 33, schoolteacher*

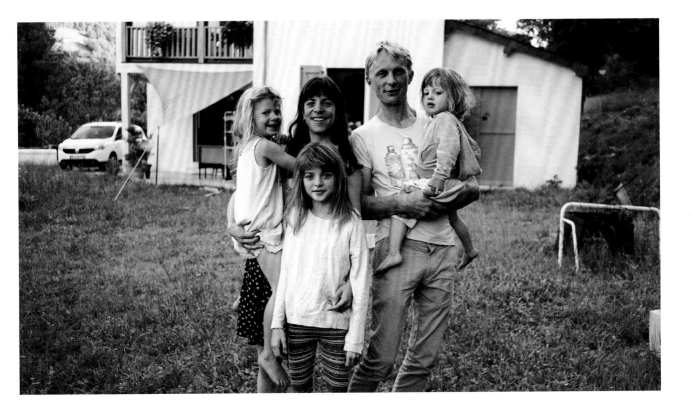

# ALIVE

*Hirel, Ille-et-Vilaine*

My last relationship lasted four years, but at the end, the routine became awful. I no longer wanted to make her feel alive, like I did before.

I am doing all right being single until I find the right girl. You have to be a little bit macho in order to seduce a girl. Not in your words, but in your attitude. You have to seem inaccessible; you have to show that you are strong, but not too much.

At the moment, I am seeing two girls, and I'm interested in four more.

One is a cashier I met three weeks ago in a supermarket. We looked at each other, and I felt my heart beating really hard. I went back. I had nothing to buy. So I bought a pack of beer and the July edition of *Cosmopolitan*. Because, yes, I do read girls' magazines. I think they're fun, and all the things that we, men, can't see, we can read it all in there.

I went back the next day. I bought some butter and Nutella, even though I never eat any. I wanted to give her my number, but I didn't; it didn't feel quite right.

I'm going to go back, but I have no idea what I'll buy next time.

*Nicolas Ourselin, 26, customer service representative*

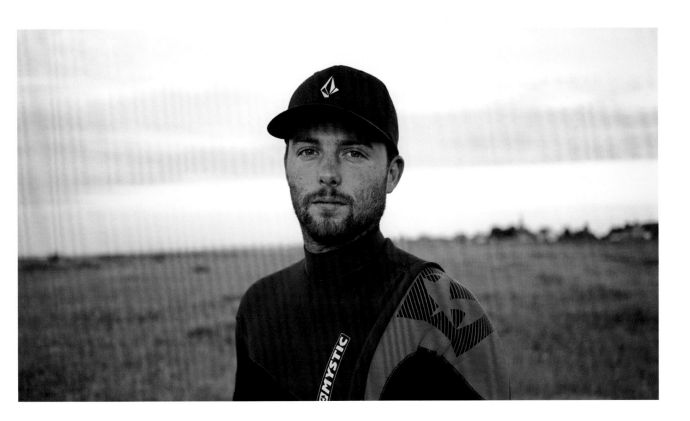

# COUCH

*Clermont-l'Hérault, Hérault*

People always say men are cruel. But women can be cruel too. I was with a sadistic woman for seven years. She destroyed me.

I found myself alone. I had never been on my own. Ever. I would cry of rage because of the loneliness. My children didn't call. No one was calling. I was decomposing. And I was too much of a coward to kill myself. So I would smoke all day, wishing for a stroke.

I had one.

But I survived. And I decided that I was going to be happy. So I started recording songs. My YouTube channel has more than four hundred videos now. "L'Hymne à l'amour" by Edith Piaf.

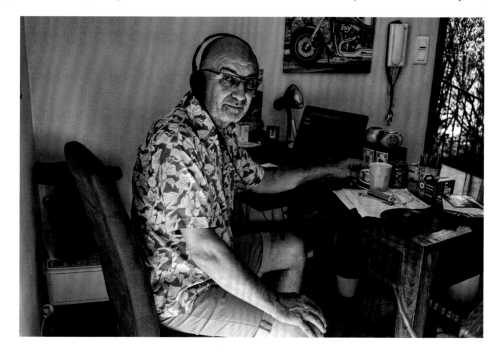

"I Will Always Love You" by Whitney Houston. I love singing women's songs with a deep voice, the voice of a man hurting inside.

I found a job too. I am the man who picks up the phone when you order that appliance you just saw on TV, and I am signed up on a teleoperator platform. My profile pic is me singing with a mic. One day, I got a message from Christelle, another teleoperator: "So you are a singer?"

We started talking. Then calling each other. She lived 280 miles away. We invented our universe. A place where we were happy. I would tell her: "Come with me. Let's have a coffee at the bar next door." We had imagined the owner, his love life. Then she would say: "Come with me. Let's rest for a bit in front of the fireplace."

After four months, I asked: "Want to come over?" When she arrived, we cooked, we sat down on the couch. Watched videos. I told her I spent half my days on my couch. I wasn't ashamed. That is how I live.

Two months ago, she moved in.

We both work from home now. I am in the living room, and she is in the bedroom. When one of us reaches ten sales, we stop for a second and kiss.

She doesn't talk much. She is a silent one. But I am not asking for more. I don't need an all-consuming passion.

But I am also scared. Because I know it can end.

*Candido Cabrejas, 58, sales representative*

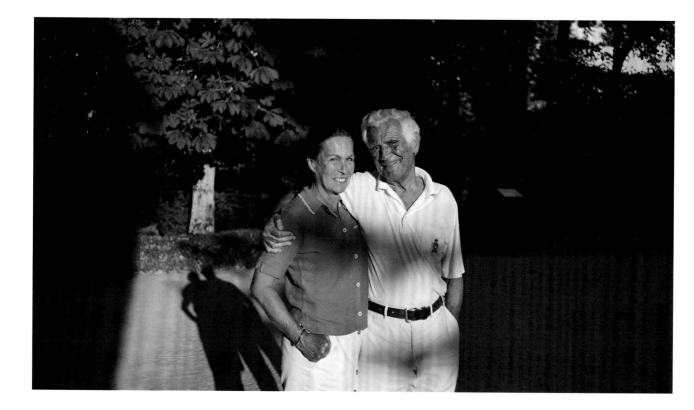

# Newlyweds

*Salignac-Eyvigues, Dordogne*

I had been divorced for four years.

I had always been friends with Patrick, but I had lost touch with him for ten years. I called him after a friend said she had bumped into him.

He was a confirmed bachelor. He had even tried to seduce me when I was married!

There was no way I was going to be with him. But he was my friend so I organized a dinner for him with a few single, rich women, hurting for love. During that dinner, we didn't have much time to talk, so I asked him if he wanted to go out, just the two of us. I said this with no hidden agenda.

After dinner, he told me he was feeling sad and asked to spend the night at my house. I had a boyfriend at the time, but I had no idea where he was. Patrick was very insistent. I said okay, and I put a pillow between us. He promised not to touch me. What a liar! The kiss was so amazing. I just told myself: "Come on, old lady, let loose. Who knows what tomorrow holds?"

He went crazy after that. He would send flowers to my workplace every day, as if we were newlyweds. My office was covered in so many flowers.

We never left each other.

When we reconnected, he was sixty and I was fifty. I'm his first wife. He had never found love or a soul mate. He had a very bad image of women. He always thought they were after his money. And he would get bored quite fast. He needed tenderness. So did I.

What we had—it grew into something strong.

Also, we had the same past. It's easier to change lives when you are young than when you are older. But I knew his friends. And he knew mine. He was really good friends with my ex-husband. That was the condition for me to get remarried: my next husband had to be in harmony with my past life. It's unbearable for me to erase the past.

Today, we are a rather amazing reconstructed

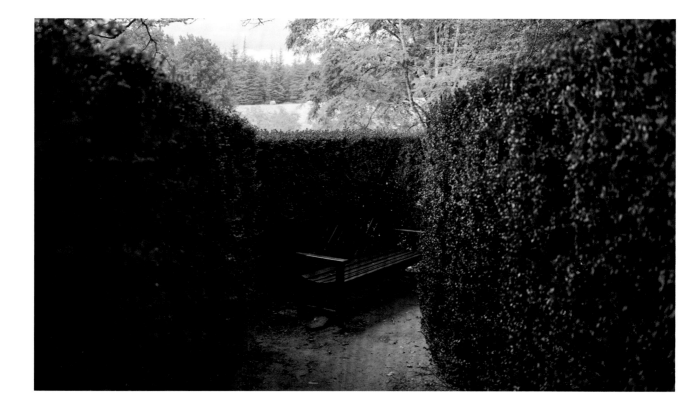

Newlyweds

family. We spend our holidays with my ex-husband and his wife, and we often have dinner together. All the barriers have fallen; there's no jealousy, no acrimony. Patrick tells me that my ex-husband is now his best friend.

I have two men in my life: the father of my children and my second husband, who I married eleven years ago. The circle is closed.

*Capucine Sermadiras de Pouzols de Lile, 62,*
*and Patrick Sermadiras de Pouzols de Lile, 71,*
*owners of the Eyrignac Manor Gardens*

# Exhausted

*Serverette, Lozère*

My ex-husband was an alcoholic. When he drank, he would break everything in the house. I was so scared of him. No one wanted to see him anymore, but I stayed.

One day, my daughter was almost finished with her summer camp. She told her counselors that she didn't want to go home because she was terrified of her father. Social workers got involved. My kids couldn't be with their dad on their own anymore. When I had work meetings after school hours, I would have to take them with me in the car, and I would park under a window to see them from where I was sitting. That was the trigger for me. I filed for divorce.

And I met Vincent. We knew each other. I liked him. He liked me. I knew it. But he wouldn't make a move. He wasn't much of a talker. He was a loner. Never married. No kids. I was thinking: "How am I possibly going to get him?" But one day, out of the blue, he kissed me. Yes!

After the chaos I had gone through, I was exhausted. I wasn't looking for the handsome man; I was looking for security and tranquility. Vincent was exactly that. I fell in love with him. With the quiet. I needed it. The dead calm.

He relieved me from all my anguish. He made me feel so human again.

He was an amazing stepfather. He took us all into his house. And it was difficult. My kids were teenagers, and really, they were not easy to deal with. If I had been in his shoes, I would have run away immediately. But he didn't. He took care of them.

Sometimes, I would like him to talk more. When we go to the restaurant, I do my monologues. I would like him to surprise me. But he doesn't.

He loves motorbikes. I hate them. I love hiking. He'd rather go to the gym. But it doesn't matter. He is my pillar.

When I was with my ex-husband, I never knew in what state I would find him when I got home from work. I was always anxious about going home. Now, I'm not afraid. I am happy to go home.

When I was with my ex-husband, sex was brutal. I hated it. I would ask him to be more tender. I would say no. But I was his wife, and I had to do what he wanted.

With Vincent, we make love.

*Odile Martel, 56, tax auditor, and Vincent Vadelorge, 56, unemployed*

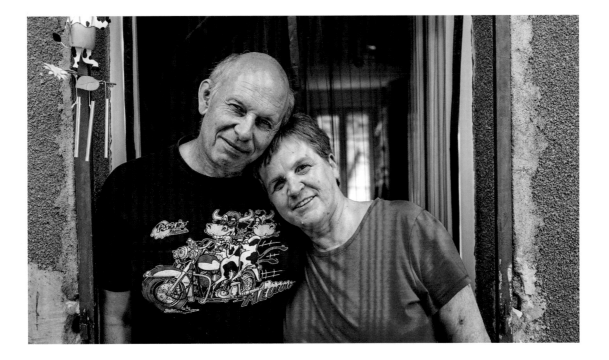

# PRINCESS

*Landerneau, Finistère*

I left my husband eleven months ago.

At the beginning, I was in robot mode, taking care of all the papers. But in the last two months, I realized that I am truly alone. I have two great kids, a lot of friends, and students. I am never by myself, yet I feel lonely.

I never understood why girls or guys would quickly get back into new relationships right after a breakup. Now I do.

That passionate love—I don't believe in it. Or it's only ephemeral. It doesn't last. My ex is still sending me messages. The love he is writing about is idyllic. It's literary love. He is in love with love. But not with a real person. He is in love with Victor Hugo and Chateaubriand. It's destructive. My ex-husband doesn't love me. He worships an idealized image of me. But I will always love him.

He will always be a part of me. And I will always worry about him.

But it's hard. I am afraid of never being loved again. It's easier to say that I prefer to be alone, but do I really have a choice? Will someone want to be with me? That fear really haunts me. So I do things on my own now. I went to a concert alone the other day. I don't need a crutch anymore.

I'm a schoolteacher, and I read stories with the kids. They always scream at the end: "They got married and lived happily ever after!" It would be nice to read a story where Cinderella and her prince divorce at the end. It would be closer to reality. What about a tale where he divorces Cinderella and then hooks up with Snow White?

*Laëtitia Le Bis, 47, schoolteacher*

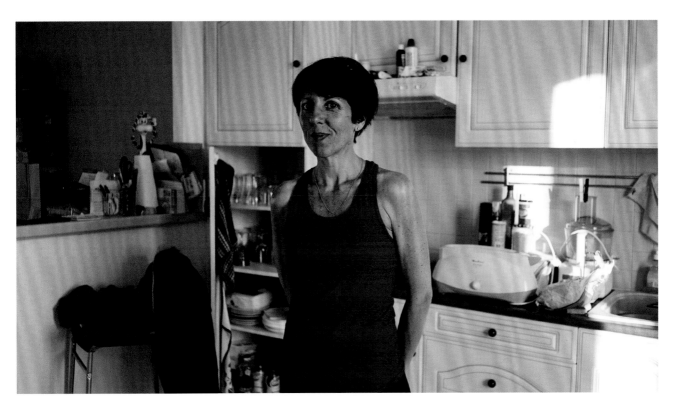

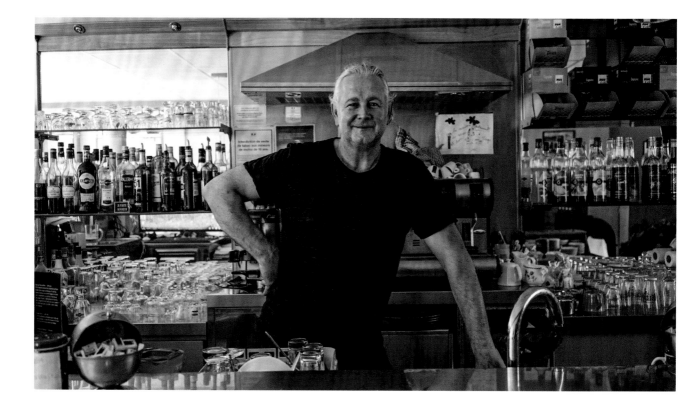

# ALONE

*Barret-sur-Méouge, Hautes-Alpes*

I was married once. But that was twenty-two years ago. Since then, I've always been chasing love. Chasing, chasing, chasing love. But I've always been disappointed.

I have always been in love with the passion. I never wanted my romance to be bland. I have never wanted to go slowly. No. I never doubted myself. Ever. I gave each woman everything. Trips. Money. My soul.

But it never worked. It would last three weeks, one month.

So I have had a lot of women, not because I wanted to have lots of sex, but because I was ready to try again. With another woman. Again. And again.

But I was disappointed. Again. And again.

I chose them too young. Too pretty.

I have no regrets.

I am dating my waitress now. She is thirty-two. I am fifty-four. But it's not working, so we are just letting it go. Little by little.

I have always counted in twos. Even when I was single, I would always buy a second ticket for a trip or a concert, because I always hoped I would go with someone. I always used to have a knot in my throat when it was over with a girl. "She" was always the one; "she" is not anymore.

I am going to do something I have never done before. I am going to travel alone. I've planned a trip to Paris, Vienna, London, and Lisbon.

One ticket. Not two.

I am scared.

*Marc Bernard, 54, owner of the restaurant*
*L'Auberge de la Méouge*

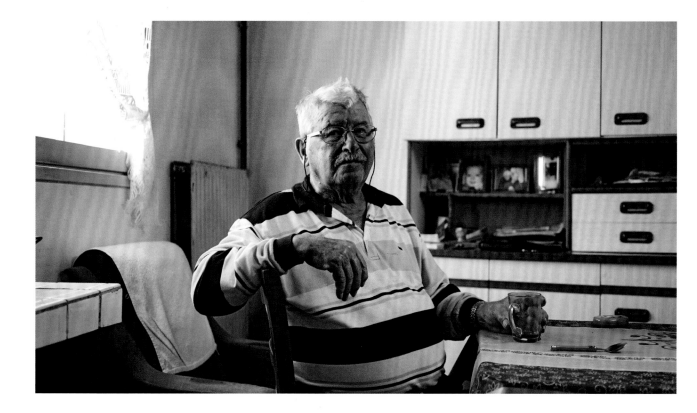

# ASLEEP

*Saint-Orens-Pouy-Petit, Gers*

I lost my wife last November. Her name was Marie-Jeanne. I met her at a village ball.

We didn't live in the same town. I would write her letters all the time so we could meet up every weekend. I would talk to her about mundane things; if I had a cold, for instance. I would write that I kissed her tenderly. She was a simple girl, just like me. A girl from the countryside.

We were together for forty-seven years. I loved her. Marriage is like a business. I built the house. She cooked and raised the children. One of them is mentally disabled. He lives in an assisted-living center. When they told him his mother had died, he cried. I thought that when he came back to the house, he would look for her everywhere, open the doors, like he used to do. But he didn't. He didn't ask for her. He knew.

She is buried in the cemetery down in the village. I still have to put her stone marker with her name, the year she was born, and the year she died. I am also going to add a little cross.

There are moments when I really get depressed, when I am really low. *Oh là là*, you can't even imagine. I miss her.

She was a good cook because she was from the Landes region, where there are a lot of good cooks.

In the winter, we would watch television, then sit near the fire and fall asleep in our respective chairs. We were happy. I always hoped it would last forever. It didn't.

Please forgive me if I cry.

*Lucien Lalanne, 81, retired mason*

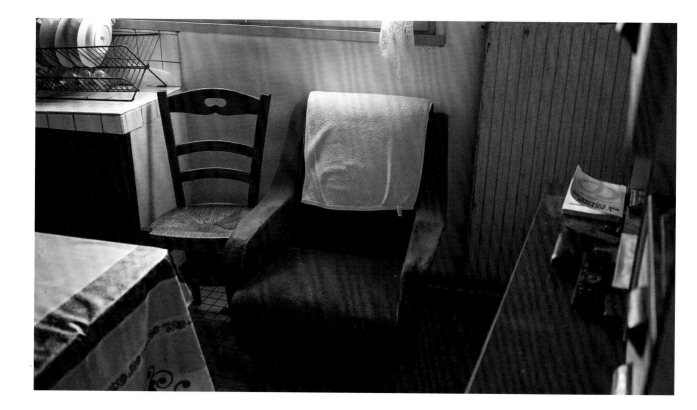

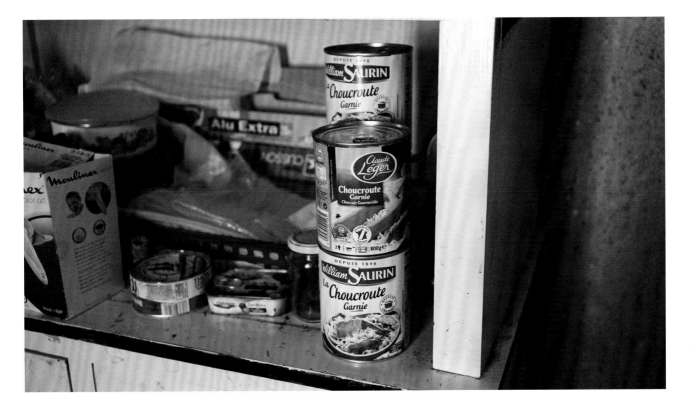

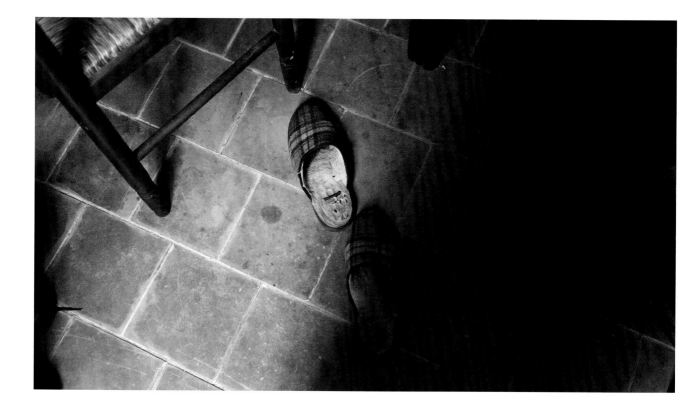

ASLEEP

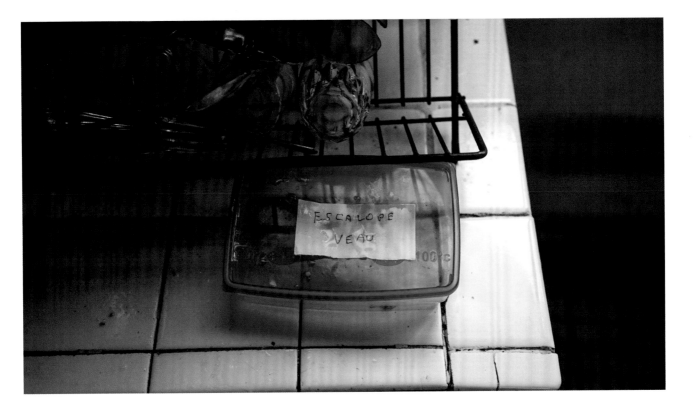

# Answers

*Venelles, Bouches-du-Rhône*

It was early summer. I was preparing for the start of the school year on our computer, and I downloaded a document. I couldn't find it anymore so I looked for it, and I ended up seeing a file with the name of one of my husband's colleagues on it. I opened it. And there it was, all the emails they had exchanged.

He had saved every single one of them.

I went to lie down. I sent him a text: "You can leave me."

He came home. We made love. And the next day, he was gone.

She was young. I was old. She had an interesting job. I was a teacher. She was smart. I wasn't. She was pretty. I was ugly. I couldn't compete with her.

My husband and I had met thirty-five years earlier. I came from a bourgeois family who voted Conservative. His parents were communists, and he loved adventure. I read novels. He read newspapers. He knew so much more than I did. I admired him.

But whatever I did or said was never good enough. Never an "I love you." Neither to me nor to our children. Never a compliment. But maybe he just didn't know how to do it because no one had ever taught him.

I wanted to leave him. So many times. But I didn't. I always ended up convincing myself I was wrong. That he was nice. That he had raised the children well. That after this long, this was probably just what love was like. So I thought our life was normal.

Six months after he left me, he left a voice mail on my phone. He was crying. She had left him. "I am such a fool. You were right." You cannot imagine how many times I have listened to that message.

So we got back together.

It's been three years. He's never moved back home. I am still waiting. I am still taking antidepressants. I don't know if I've forgiven him. I still ask him why he left me. He told me I was as guilty as he was, because I hadn't tried to hold him back.

He still doesn't tell me he loves me. He tells me he has affection for me. He tells me I should leave him.

But I take what there is to take. I have no choice. It's him or nothing. How do I know if this is love?

*Valérie Vindiolet, 57, schoolteacher*

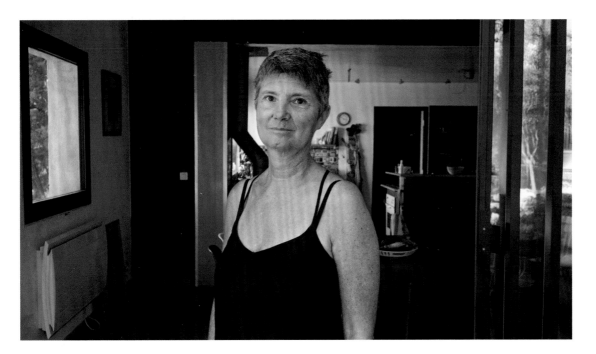

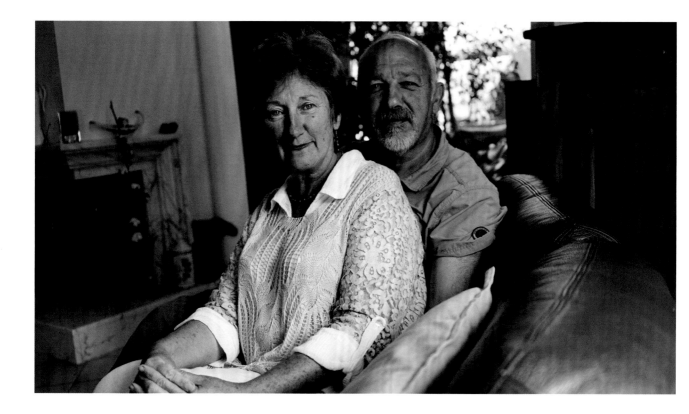

# CLOGS

*Orléans, Loiret*

It was the first day of school. She was sixteen. I was seventeen. The first thing I noticed were her shoes. We were wearing the exact same wooden clogs. Then, I saw her eyes. Something between fearlessness and insolence. We started writing each other letters. We would exchange them after class, read them at night, and share new letters in the morning.

We have been together for forty-two years. I have the same emotions as I had for her when I was a kid. She will never give up on me. She is a rebel, and she never has set any limits on me. It is very hard to talk about her because I usually talk about "us." We made Hervé and Isabelle. We are not standing side by side; we are one.

I haven't told her I loved her lately. But I tell many people that I love her. To her, no. I'd rather show it. A hug. A kiss. Flowers.

We still make love. But not as much as we used to—Isabelle has lymphatic disease. And it's something we still don't speak much about. We should.

There is this song where the lyrics go: "I like to lock myself up with you. Close the door and think of nothing." And it makes me cry. It makes me think of those days where Isabelle and I would escape somewhere and make love.

When I was seventeen, I would look at her with marvel and think: "Why did she pick me?" I am the same way today; I still wonder.

*Hervé Robbes, 59, and Isabelle Robbes, 58, hypnotherapists*

# ACKNOWLEDGMENTS

When I started this journey, I had no idea where it would take me. But as soon as I started traveling, the beauty happened: I met the most extraordinary people—most of whom became my friends. Each one of them shared their stories with me. And each one of them healed me. With words, with kindness. Through their love. Forever, I will be grateful to them. Thank you. *Merci.*

One year later, I flew to New York to meet Ann Godoff and Patrick Nolan at Penguin Books. A couple months later, I took a train to London to meet Isabel Wall and Rose Poole at Viking. What warmth. I thank the four of them—so much—for taking me on board. My very first book. Casey Denis, Alicia Cooper, Claire Vaccaro, Nancy Bernhaut Scott at Penguin Press, and on the other side of the pond, Sara Granger and Holly Ovenden at Viking, worked so hard to put together this book. I am tremendously grateful to them. Their energy and their enthusiasm were boundless. Same goes to my two wonderful publicists: Colleen Boyle and Sapphire Rees.

Thank you also to my crack team of agents, Susanna Lea in New York, Mark Kessler in Paris, and Kerry Glencorse in London for making it all happen.

But this book would never have been possible without my friend Gaëlle Faure. She was there for me from day one, editing all my stories and giving me invaluable feedback. Hélène Goupil, Estelle Koenig, Gaëlle Fichet, Margaux Le Gouvello, Dara Kerr, Laura Wenus, Valentine de Panafieu, Ariane Bernard, Clotilde Dominguez, Claudia Escobar, Tayo Heuser, and Clément Fromentin were also always there to help me, editing stories and giving me advice—anytime, anywhere. They have my deepest affection.

Thank you to my amazing crew of transcribers, whose hard work ensured I would have the most precise records of my conversations: Alexis Danan, Alicia Berard, Oona O'Brien, Muriel Bravo, Marie Goullieux, Gabrielle Franck, Daniel Hoffman, Patricia Neves, Elena Toth, Eric Spring, Olivier Nguyen, Valérie Cordy, Pierre-Emmanuelle De Leusse, and Camil Aissani Pache. And thank you to Jean-Philippe Gras, who designed a beautiful book proposal.

I particularly want to thank the *New York Times*'s video team, and specifically Justine Simons, who recruited me as an intern, as well as all the many editors and colleagues who have shown faith in my work all these years.

When I called Kerri McDonald, social photo editor at the *New York Times*, to tell her I was about to wander around France to search for love, she instantly believed in my project and was the first person to publish my stories from the road. Then came Lucy Conticello, my friend and photo editor at *Le Monde*, who introduced me to Clara Georges and Eric Collier. They fell in love with the work and gave me a full page in the newspaper every other weekend for a full year. And one day, while I was eating duck in the Gers after a month of traveling, I got a phone call from

Florence Martin-Kessler from *Live Magazine*, who invited me onstage to talk about love. It was a beautiful experience.

There are many people who helped me fuel up while I was writing this book and thank goodness for them. The Zéphyr and Culbuto cafés for all the morning macchiatos, the Jourdain and Nagawa restaurants for the delicious meals, and JLPhoto for printing out all my transcripts. And the Chamois d'Or hotel in Cordon, where I hibernated to finish the book.

I also want to thank my family: Chilla, Patrick, Luc-Henry, Nadine, my grandmother Maria, my aunts, uncles, and cousins whom I love dearly. Viva the "Heuser life."

Finally, there are two people that have always stood by me: Lydia Chávez and Mimi Chakarova. They were my professors at the UC Berkeley School of Journalism, then became my mentors, and they are now my best friends. They taught me to trust myself, to trust my work—and are at the genesis of this journey. Who would I be without you? Thank you.